COMPANY GRADE

©2015 Henry "Rocky" Colavita

Published by Hellgate Press

(An imprint of L&R Publishing, LLC)

Hellgate Press
PO Box 3531
Ashland, OR 97520
email: info@hellgatepress.com

Editor: Harley B. Patrick
Cover Design: L. Redding

Cataloging In Publication Data is available from the publisher upon request.

Printed and bound in the United States of America
First edition 10 9 8 7 6 5 4 3 2 1

To all my Vietnam Veteran Brothers

CONTENTS

COMPANY GRADE

Memoir of an Angry Skipper

HENRY 'ROCKY' COLAVITA

Preface

I KNOW FROM THE MANY REUNIONS I HAVE ATTENDED with former soldiers of Delta Company, 2/8 Cav, that we don't all agree on the details of the combat experiences we shared. For example, at several of our reunions one of my former troopers continues to ask, "Skipper, remember that gook we threw out of the chopper?" I swear, we never threw anyone out of a chopper. In fact, what I remember about the few prisoners we did take was, as soon as they were secured and no longer a threat to us, my soldiers offered them cigarettes and some of the tastiest items from the C Ration boxes, like the peaches or pound cake. Prisoners were never in our custody very long since the intelligence types from higher headquarters couldn't wait to meet them. In that regard, we did put POWs on helicopters in the custody of others and I do not believe for a minute that any of them got thrown out.

Over the years since Vietnam, I have written many letters on behalf of my soldiers to help them get combat awards they should have received but didn't, mostly with a favorable outcome. Another type of letter I have written for my soldiers is in support of their claims for Veterans Administration (VA) compensation for PTSD. This letter describes a gruesome or traumatic incident or event in which the soldier was involved contributing to his

PTSD. After one of our reunions I wrote such a letter for one of my soldiers who told me he was still deeply troubled since he found the head of an unfortunate soldier who was blown to bits on LZ Rita one night by a mysterious explosion. One or two reunions later, another soldier asked for such a letter telling me he was the one who found the dead soldier's head. The deceased soldier actually left enough body parts on the LZ that I sincerely believe neither one of those soldiers was untruthful and both had found a trauma inducing piece of human anatomy. I wrote a letter for him also.

I am sure after my book is published and I let my guys know about it, many of them will want to get it and bring it with them to a reunion, at which time I'll be happy to sign their copy. But I am also sure some will write or call me or tell me at that next reunion, "Skipper, that wasn't the way that incident went down." Or, "That happened on LZ Carolyn, not Rita," or, such and such "… happened a week later than you wrote." However, this is my military memoir and, that being the case, the only recollection that counts here is mine!

I am also sure there will be hurt feelings for some of my combat brothers whom I didn't mention by name. The fact is, with incoming replacements due to tour completions caused either by normal DEROS or by enemy action, easily two hundred or more soldiers were with me in Delta Company. They will have to be satisfied knowing that they are my brothers and I love them.

One

To Be a Soldier

I HAVE NO IDEA AT WHAT AGE KIDS DEVELOP a functioning memory. The earliest thing I can remember, however, was my family living in a small place that I would later decide was an apartment. The only thing I remember about living in that apartment was one night my parents turned off the lights, closed the curtains and we just hung out in the dark. I don't remember listening to any sounds but as I got older I noticed a big console radio and I supposed we may have listened to it with the lights out. Years later I asked my dad about that night and he told me it was called a blackout. He said, "We were at war with the Japanese and the Germans and we turned the lights off at night so they can't see us to bomb us." Since World War II ended in 1945 and I was born in 1941 my recollections of the blackout had to as a baby or toddler. Many years later in the age of the Internet, I queried Wikipedia about WW II and mandatory blackouts in and around New York City. I learned that there were no real blackouts but there were occasional practice blackouts in the event getting bombed became a real threat.

Other than our apartment dwelling blackout, my real memories began while we lived in a large house on Franklin Avenue in Belleville, New Jersey. I remember walking to Catechism class in a big catholic church down the street in Nutley. I also knew that my father was a soldier. As time went by, I became aware that he was an officer, a captain. I knew that, except on Saturdays and Sundays, he left the house each morning, got into our 1942 Chevrolet sedan and went to work at a place called Fort Hamilton in New York City. I couldn't wait for him to come home in the evenings because he would let me wear his officer's hat. I didn't have to worry about competition from my older brother Frank because he didn't care anything about our dad's Army hat or uniform. "Frank, do you want to wear dad's hat?" "No! I don't want to wear that dumb hat." Dad actually had two hats, both round with a bill and chin strap. One was dark brown to be worn with the winter dress uniform and the other was Khaki and was worn with the summer uniform. Many years later I found out that those hats are sarcastically called flying saucer hats by the U. S. Army Airborne and that type of hat would never be worn by paratroopers. My dad didn't see any action during WW II. He was assigned to the Transportation Corps but he also had a law degree and maybe that's what kept him out of combat. His older brother Mike did get into the war fighting the Germans. Uncle Mike was now a police officer with the Newark, New Jersey Police Department. Going to visit my dad's parents, usually every Sunday for spaghetti, was pretty strange because we were always told we had to be very quiet.

The reason for this was because Uncle Mike worked the night shift so he slept during the day, and my dad's younger brother, Uncle Eddie, played piano in a night club so he also slept during the day. On the rare occasions when we visited grandma and grandpa and Uncle Mike was awake, he was happy to show us the German helmet and dagger souvenirs he brought back from Europe. As a former soldier and now police officer, Uncle Mike was my hero. As for Uncle Eddie the piano player, he was okay, although I never actually heard him play.

Soon after I started the second grade, my mother told Frank and I that our dad was being transferred to Hawaii. The year was 1948 and by that time Frank and I had a little brother named Billy. Mom said Hawaii was a group of islands far out in the Pacific Ocean. Dad was gone soon after Mom said he was leaving and we were to follow as soon as he had a place for us to live. I remember a long trip by train across country which ended with us staying temporarily at Fort Mason, a small military post in San Francisco. The fort overlooked a rocky island called Alcatraz. We didn't get to know Fort Mason or Alcatraz very well because before long, we were on a ship headed for Hawaii. After a long trip, during which we all got a good dose of sea sickness, we found ourselves living in a four family row house on an Army installation named Schofield Barracks on the Hawaiian Island of Oahu. From the front door of our unit we could clearly see a huge white cross sitting high up between mountain peaks. The area between the peaks was called the Kolekole Pass and the cross, we were told, marked the spot where the Japanese planes crossed over the island on their way to bomb Pearl Harbor.

I went to school on Schofield Barracks and we visited nearby Pearl Harbor a few times. Much of it was still in the process of being rebuilt after the Japanese attack and plenty of wreckage was still as it had been after the bombs and torpedoes did their work. The U.S.S. *Arizona* was not yet a national memorial but she was clearly visible sitting on the harbor bottom. I don't know how long we lived on Schofield Barracks but one day mom told us dad was being transferred and we would be moving to a smaller post called Fort Ruger on the other side of the island. I liked Schofield, my school and the friends I had made. I was not happy about the move and I was particularly upset that I wouldn't be seeing the Kolekole cross any more. I don't know why I was so fond of it, other than I was Catholic and it was a cross. Years later my son Christopher, then a captain in the Army, received orders assigning him to the 25th Infantry Division at Schofield Barracks. "Chris," I asked him, "when you get to Schofield, I want you to check out the big white cross on the Kolekole Pass." (I had three sons but like my own family with three boys, he was the only one interested in the military). I gave him a while to settle in before asking him by email about the cross but it wasn't until after the September 11, 2001 attack by Al Qaeda that he had a chance to look for my cross. He reported that no one he talked with knew anything about the cross. He said he drove up to the Pass to see what he could find out about it but after 9/11, the road had been closed to nonessential traffic. Apparently there is significant ammunition storage in that area and access is now limited only to those on official business. Although Chris was assigned to Schofield Barracks, he did not have any official business in the area of the Kolekole Pass. He did talk to a security guard, an older gentleman who appeared to Chris to be a native Hawaiian, and the guard told him he remembered hearing about the big white cross but didn't know whether or not it really existed. I was disappointed to hear this and was beginning to wonder if I had imagined the cross.

At the time Chris was stationed at Schofield, the movie "Pearl Harbor" was being shot on location and I asked him about it. He said a number of military personnel had gotten parts in the movie as extras and that's all he knew about it. I looked forward to seeing this movie. When I finally did see it I was terribly disappointed since it turned out to be a love story and not a war movie. Then one day in a video store, I picked up the DVD,

"Tora, Tora, Tora." A better moving picture about Pearl Harbor, indeed. The movie was also shot on location in 1970 and I was particularly happy to note that, in the movie, as the planes of the Empire of Japan were flying over the Kolekole Pass, a giant white cross is clearly visible standing on the mountain between the peaks.

My dad's job changed when we moved to the little Army post named Fort Ruger, several miles away from Schofield Barracks. Although he wore the insignia of the Army Transportation Corps, his new job was as the Officer In Charge (OIC) of the post Officers' Club, which was named The Cannon Club. I quickly got over being upset about leaving Schofield because living on Fort Ruger proved to be a lot more fun than Schofield Barracks. We moved into a four family structure exactly like the one we lived in at Schofield. Fort Ruger was built on the side of the extinct volcano named Diamond Head. It was high enough up on the Honolulu side of the crater that from our front door we could see half-way across the entire island of Oahu. Without the glass and aluminum structures along Waikiki Beach and inland which would later block this view, we could clearly see another extinct volcano crater called Punchbowl. This crater housed the National Memorial Cemetery of the Pacific. In the evening, the lights of downtown Honolulu were spectacular. I visited the Punchbowl crater as a kid with my parents and later during two different visits to Oahu to visit son Chris and his family.

The Cannon Club was also on the side of Diamondhead, a bit higher up the crater, giving club patrons an even better view of Honolulu. The swimming pool was just outside the bar area of the club and the pool patio served as the jumping off point from which we Army brats began our almost daily climbs to the top of Diamond Head. We traveled many times around the whole perimeter of the crater enjoying the view for 360 degrees. The highest point of the crater, seen so often in postcards and movies, was scary to cross but we did it regularly. Observation bunkers and gun emplacements were installed in this high point of the crater. Down inside the crater were rifle ranges and other military training facilities. Although these rifle ranges were no longer used by troops stationed on Fort Ruger, we kids filled the vacuum by shooting BB guns at tin cans, and each other. The side of the crater facing out to sea had tunnels running from the inside of the crater to the outside, complete with railroad tracks to roll large guns, which were no longer there, to the outside edge of the crater which could then fire on enemy aircraft and landing craft.

On my first trip to visit my son and his family in Hawaii after I retired from my second career with the Fairfax County, Virginia, Sheriff's Office, I saw that Diamond Head is now a state monument and the opportunity for kids to have their way with the crater, as we did in the late forties and early fifties, was no longer possible. On this first visit Chris and I were driving to Diamond Head along the highway which passes in front of Waikiki Beach. After following the left-hand curve of the road away from the beach, I saw Chris put his right turn signal on and I asked him why. He pointed to a sign with an arrow pointing to the right which said, "Diamond Head State Monument." I asked him to flick off the blinker and go straight. He did and within seconds I saw on the left side of the street a grocery store with a sign that read, "Sun Ray Market." "Chris," I said all excited, "I used to walk to that market from our quarters to get bread and milk." Seconds later we passed between the two long neglected stone gate guard posts which used to mark the entrance to Fort Ruger. The long four family row houses on the hill to our right were gone but the concrete slabs they were built on remained, including the one our company grade quarters stood on. Higher on the Diamond Head crater sat The Cannon Club. We took a hard right turn and stopped to explore the location of the housing units and the club. Both were overgrown with weeds and were posted with signs saying, "No Trespassing." We did a little trespassing and I knew this real estate was far too valuable not to be used for luxury condos, high rise hotels and the like. The old Cannon Club itself was plastered with signs declaring that it was owned by the City and County of Honolulu. We drove through more of what used to be the fort. The building which used to be the post movie theater was now a stage for the local community theater. All that I was seeing brought back memories, all of them were good. The parade field which used to be surrounded with field grade officer living quarters was now overtaken by a community college campus. Just up from what used to be the post movie theater, which was actually separated from the post by a public roadway, was an old tuberculosis sanatorium. Back then, military kids who lived on post and attended the Honolulu Public School, Aliiolani Elementary, had to walk past this building to get there. We were told by the older kids that we needed to hold our breath as we passed this building so we wouldn't get TB and we all did that. The old building was still standing and it still appeared to be some sort of medical facility. Chris was a bit amazed by my memory but we came here to visit the crater so we turned around so I could renew my friendship with Diamond Head. Of course, now we had to buy tickets.

So from 1948 to 1952 my family and I lived in paradise, thanks to the Army. After about a year living in the row houses for company grade officers, my father was promoted to major and we were entitled to field grade officer's quarters.

We moved the mile or so to duplex housing located around the post parade field. Much nicer housing and still within walking distance of the officers' club pool. Along with the promotion, my dad left behind his duties as OIC of The Cannon Club and assumed some desk job at Fort Shafter a few miles away, at the Headquarters of the U.S. Army Pacific Command. Again, what was not to like. Soldiers frequently held outdoor classes on the parade field near our home. While the soldiers sat on the grass for instructional sessions, M-1 Garand rifles and M1 carbines were stacked nearby and since all the kids in the area were children of officers, no one said a thing as we walked among the stacked rifles, some of us hoping one day to command our own soldiers. For four wonderful years we lived in paradise on an Army post. I made good friends living around that parade ground. We frequently played war on the lava rocks behind our quarters and, I guess because of where we lived, our enemy was always the Japanese and never the Germans. At 1700 hours each day the Military Police lowered the Post flag located just off the parade ground while we kids stood at attention and saluted. But, all good things must come to an end. In the summer of 1952 my father received orders sending us to Virginia. Looking back on my own Army career, I am sorry I never had a chance to get myself stationed in paradise.

TWO

Discovery and Decision

W E SETTLED INTO A BRAND NEW THREE BEDROOM house in Arlington County, Virginia, not far from my father's job at the Office of the Chief of Transportation next to National Airport. Our house was in an all new housing development and all the kids living there recently moved here from somewhere else. We were all making new friends at the same time. Arlington County is the home of the Pentagon, Fort Myer, Arlington Hall Station, at that time, and other military agencies scattered throughout. My new neighborhood was full of military brats. I was able to walk to my new elementary school, Nottingham, only about two blocks away. I had been a Cub Scout most of my time in Hawaii and had graduated to the Boy Scouts just before we returned to the mainland. I intended to stay with the Scouts but none of my new sixth grade classmates were scouts and, if I mentioned scouting to any of them, it became apparent to me that no one was interested. I was disappointed at first but there was so much new territory and stuff to explore, and new friends to be made, that I didn't miss scouting for long. At that time I was a pretty good student and didn't mind going to class at Nottingham or even doing homework, with the exception of arithmetic. Problems with math and numbers in general would be a lifelong struggle for me.

Seventh grade was a complete mess. All the kids in my development were to be among the first students in the new Williamsburg Junior High School, also two blocks walking distance from my house, but in another direction, but it was still under construction and wouldn't be finished for another year. So for seventh grade, we were all bussed to an underutilized elementary school several miles away where we did half the day, and then walked in a group a few blocks to where we did the second half of the day in Stratford Junior High School. The real Stratford students seemed quite put out with our apparent disruptive presence in their building and when Williamsburg is completed, these two schools will be fierce athletic competitors for the next two years, at least as fierce as thirteen- and fourteen-year-old kids can be. At the end of the ninth grade, both Stratford and Williamsburg students will meet again as classmates in Washington-Lee High School in north Arlington County. Then our fierce athletic rival will be Wakefield High in south Arlington.

Williamsburg did open in time for the eighth grade and once again I was able to walk to school.

In Virginia, boys team sports begin in junior high but the choices are limited to football, basketball, baseball and track and field. As a somewhat undersized kid, I didn't see football or basketball as options for me. Baseball was also out because I simply didn't care for that sport. I thought baseball was boring. But track and field was my choice and I discovered that I was faster than most kids. My other big discovery, after talking with other Army brats who wanted to attend the U. S. Military Academy at West Point (USMA), followed by careers in the Army, was that my chances of getting into and graduating from the Academy were not good. West Point had no curriculum resembling liberal arts. All cadets were in an engineering oriented curriculum with heavy doses of advanced math. I not only hated math, I was now scared of it. I believe this stemmed from an incident in ninth grade algebra when this particularly nasty math teacher sent me to the board to solve an algebraic equation in front of the class. I was unable to do it and I was humiliated. Perhaps that teacher wouldn't have picked me for this task if she had known I was going to grow up to be a trained killer. I began to think seriously about turning my running ability into a track scholarship at a liberal arts college which had an Army Reserve Officer Training Corps (ROTC) program.

I was always very loyal to my vision of becoming an Army officer but I did have some second thoughts while growing up in Arlington. A new neighbor moved in across the street from us. This neighbor was a sergeant with the Arlington County Police Department. I'm sorry to say that just because he was a policeman, some kids in the neighborhood didn't like him and played pranks on him whenever they thought they could get away with it. Once, while the sergeant and his wife were on vacation, these kids put a "For Sale" sign in their yard. Also, the sergeant did appear a bit overweight so the kids who didn't like him nicknamed him "The Fat Cop." I personally liked this police officer and I think he liked me and knew I wasn't one of the pranksters, but I never did rat out any of the kids who were, mainly because my brother Frank was one of them. In addition to the sergeant, around the corner and up the hill lived an Arlington police major. The major rated a take home car, a black, unmarked sedan with red emergency lights peeking out from the grille. Another police officer who had a take home car lived a couple of blocks away also. Arlington County is relatively small, as counties go, at only twenty-six square miles to include the six hundred and twenty-four acres of Arlington National Cemetery. With the requirement at that time that County police officers live in the county, almost everybody lived near some police officers. With my favorite uncle being both a soldier and a policeman, thoughts of my career sometimes drifted towards law enforcement. Maybe the FBI or Secret Service.

But this line of thought was always temporary. As soon as I saw a war movie or TV show about the military, my resolve to become an Army officer returned as strong as ever.

With some track records and championships accumulated while running for the Washington-Lee High School Generals, I was offered and accepted a track scholarship at Virginia Polytechnic Institute (VPI). I ran on the high school state championship mile relay two years in a row and won the Northern Virginia quarter mile championship my senior year. I came in second in the quarter mile in the state championship meet, only because I let myself get boxed in. I should have won that race. VPI believed I could help their track and field program and I was very appreciative of the scholarship. At that time, VPI was still decades away from being more famously known in collegiate athletic circles as Virginia Tech. I also had a track scholarship offer from the University of Maryland but I never seriously considered that offer for two reasons: Maryland had only an Air Force ROTC Program, and my brother Frank was there on a track scholarship. At that time in our lives I wanted to put some space between brother Frank and myself. VPI did have an Army ROTC program which would provide me with the Army officer's commission I always wanted.

Three

The Corps, The Corps
and The Corps

IN 1959, VPI WAS MOST CERTAINLY NOT A LIBERAL arts college. It was classified as a Military/Civilian institution where being in the ROTC program involved being in a cadet corps. All incoming male freshmen who were physically able were required to be in the Virginia Tech Corps of Cadets (VTCC) for their first two years. Other than for disabilities, the only exceptions to this rule was for male students who had already served in the military.

Between 1959 and 1963, VPI had a female student population of approximately three hundred; however, women were not welcome in the VTCC at that time. The VTCC was in every way similar to cadet corps at nearby Virginia Military Institute (VMI), The Citadel in Charleston, South Carolina, the Texas A&M Corps of Cadets and the USMA at West Point. As opposed to being called "plebes" like the freshmen at West Point, VPI cadet freshmen were called "rats," as is the case with our arch rival VMI eighty miles away in Lexington, Virginia. It was part of the life of a rat that any upperclassman who felt like it could stop you, force you to come to rigid attention, and then chew you out simply because he could. I really hated being chewed out by upperclassmen who were shorter than me. While the short guy was looking up my nose I could see his nasty, distorted face and he could see my eyes. Much better to be chewed out by a taller guy. I couldn't see his face due to the overhanging bill of my cadet hat, which was two fingers from the tip of my nose, and he couldn't see my eyes for the same reason.

I was fully prepared to put up with this chicken shit hazing for my first year at VPI but The Corps began interfering with my scholarship obligation to train and run. Although running cross country in the fall season was not officially a part of my scholarship, I really disliked cross country. The coach enlightened me that I didn't have to run in cross country meets if I didn't want to, but cross country training was a part of my required conditioning for indoor and outdoor track seasons in the winter and spring. I decided that if I had to practice with the cross country team, I might as well run in the meets. The problem with running and being in the corps involved all the crap I had to put up with just getting out of my barracks and to practice on time. Other freshman runners seemed to be getting to practice on time but I suspected being on scholarship was the cause of me getting my heels locked by every upperclassman between the cadet quadrangle and the practice field. To eliminate this problem the coach had me transferred from I Company, a normal cadet organization, to H Company, which was the home of the scholarship athletes. Moving to H Company did not affect the requirement to be in The Corps for a minimum of two years, but it made it a heck of a lot easier.

Upper class jocks who wanted an Army or Air Force commission, such as me and a couple of other H Company guys, had to remain in The Corps until graduation. But for H Company, being in The Corps meant only wearing the uniform to and from the Department of Military Science for ROTC classes. While in that uniform, and while wearing the white fabric belt signifying one's first year status as a rat, we were still subject to being treated like a rat by upper class members of The Corps. Once we returned to our dorm (H Company cadets shared a dormitory with upper-class jocks who were not members of The Corps,) the uniforms went in the closet and we were just like regular civilian students. Since ROTC classes were only three times a week, we were mostly civilians.

H Company was not located near the rest of the corps and was not well liked by The Corps. The exception was, if you performed well in your sport and VPI won a game, a match or a meet, then we were liked until we lost the next one. As a track athlete, I was in the minority. The population of our dorm was primarily scholarship football players. Many of them were amongst the largest human beings I had ever met. Next were scholarship basketball players, as you can imagine, the tallest, and then scholarship wrestlers, the guys with no necks.

The football players had a floating card game almost every night. One evening, one of them won big and went downtown the next day and bought a large, console color television with his winnings. For the rest of the school year, I saw that TV move from room to room every few nights. While a resident in the H Company dorm, I saw a lot of very entertaining stuff and some really dangerous stuff. The most dangerous thing I saw was the live firing of rifles and handguns, including a Ruger Blackhawk .357 magnum, from one end of the hall to the other with the round impacting on the concrete stairwell at the far end of the hall. This activity would begin with a guy with a really good set of lungs yelling, "Everybody stay in your fucking room." There was no dorm monitor or counselor assigned to keep order. I doubted that a resident monitor or counselor could have kept order. Order was supposed to be maintained by periodic visits by members of the coaching staff. It was also evident to me that only members of the football coaching staff might have been able to maintain order in this building. The tennis coach wouldn't stand a chance. I decided these visits must occur every four years because I never saw one.

One very good thing happened to me during my first days at VPI. There was a very popular homerun hitting major league baseball player with a last name of Colavito. His first name was Rocco which, of course, gave him the nickname "Rocky." My new acquaintances at school hung that nickname on me when they heard my last name, Colavita. The baseball Rocky's last name ended in "o" and mine ended in "a" but my dad always said that "o" was the masculine and "a" the feminine ending of the same family name. So, I became known as Rocky Colavita.

I much preferred being called Rocky rather than Henry and I took that nickname with me into the Army. From that point forward in my work environment, wherever that might be, I was Rocky. Back in Arlington among my old high school classmates, including at all of our reunions over the years, I again had to be Henry. One exception was for my wife, Janine, whom I married in 1970. She preferred Henry to Rocky although, as a French girl, it was pronounced, *Onri*.

****

In the late '50s and early '60s, VPI was a dismal place and so was the host town of Blacksburg. The town had one movie theater and the best place to eat when you were totally sick of the student mess hall was the restaurant in the Trailways bus station.

The student body of approximately 5,300 students was pretty equally divided between military and civilian students. Courses of study at that time were limited to engineering, agriculture and business administration. I suppose that majoring in agriculture was a possibility for me but I knew nothing about farming or raising farm animals and had no desire to learn. I selected business because it was as close as I could get to liberal arts. The business administration curriculum had only one business related math course and one accounting course. Other core subjects such as Marketing did not intimidate me and others, such as English and American History, I actually enjoyed. The business math course was taught in the freshman year and I got through it the second time around on campus. For the accounting course, also a freshman year offering, I was allowed to take it at George Washington University in D.C. the summer between my freshman and sophomore years and transfer the credits to VPI.

The only summer job I could accommodate that year was as a night janitor in a family friend's real estate and insurance businesses. These businesses occupied adjacent offices with glass front doors and humongous plate glass windows fronting on Wilson Boulevard in the Clarendon section of Arlington. Wilson Boulevard is a highly used thoroughfare only a couple of miles from Washington-Lee High School. At first, I tried to do the work after pulling the curtains closed but then the place was too dark. So, I opened the curtains wide and took my chances that no one I knew would see me on the other end of a large power buffer polishing the floor, or emptying trash cans and cleaning ashtrays. After a while I didn't care whether anyone saw me or not. *Gees, guys, did you know Henry is a janitor?* So my routine the summer of 1960 was studying for class during the day, driving to GWU in downtown Washington, D.C. for the two-hour class in the evening and then going to my janitor's job for a couple of hours, then home to bed.

But back to dismal VPI. I was actually glad it was dismal. Traveling with the track team I saw how the other half lived when we ran against party schools like the University of Virginia. It became clear to me that if I attended a "normal" college, I probably would have lost my scholarship due to drinking (two beers would knock me for a loop), and then flunk out. This motivated me to study hard, graduate, get commissioned and get on with my Army career. My sophomore year passed without any drama.

Junior year was when Army ROTC cadets would select their branch of service. I had thought all along I would choose the Transportation Corps (TC) like my father, even though it was never clear to me what he actually did. However, what my dad did would be irrelevant since I was also going to choose the Army aviation program along with the TC Branch. This would send me to flight school where I would learn to fly either helicopters or some of the slick new fixed-wing planes that belonged to the Army rather than the Air Force. As a demonstration of my determination to finish up college and get my commission, I actually maintained a B average my entire junior year and that fact was commemorated by a dark purple ribbon worn above the left breast pocket of my cadet uniform. Too bad I was wearing it for no more than two hours three days a week.

Junior year for me was a blur of studying, going to class, participating in indoor and outdoor track meets at colleges and universities all over Virginia, West Virginia, North Carolina, South Carolina with one trip to Tennessee (UT) and one to New York (USMA). I did well in my Military Science studies and picked up a designation as a Distinguished Military Student (DMS). This was important to me since there was a good possibility that with this DMS designation, I might be commissioned directly into the Regular Army (RA) rather than in the Army Reserves.

Without the DMS designation I would certainly be commissioned in the Army Reserves and have to apply separately for an RA commission. Between junior and senior years, ROTC cadets in all U.S. states and territories are required to attend a summer camp at a military installation supported by active duty Army officers and soldiers. This is a similar experience to the newly enlisted soldier's boot camp. I would be doing my summer camp at Fort Bragg, North Carolina, home of the famed 82nd Airborne Division. The camp was six weeks long and consisted of marksmanship; map reading and land navigation; serious physical training to include simulated hand-to-hand combat, survival, escape and evasion; drill and ceremonies; and the things one needed to know to be a good soldier. Things that an officer should know would be taught later in an Officer Basic Course for the branch of the Army in which the new lieutenant received his commission. Summer camp was tough but fun.

One day that was not much fun involved training in chemical agents. That day I was designated a platoon leader for our company. While listening to an NCO talk to us about the effects of different chemical agents, we were told we were going to see demonstrated how to combat the effects of certain chemical agents. For this demonstration, designated company leaders were summoned from the bleachers and issued something called an Atropine Syrette. This looked like a small tube of toothpaste but with about an inch long needle protruding from the front of the tube. The NCO demonstrated how to remove the cover over the needle, then how to numb the thigh of your choice by slapping it as hard as you can. Then, he explained the part about jamming the needle into your thigh and squeezing the contents into your upper leg. This, he informed us, would be demonstrated by the company commanders and platoon leaders. "The quicker the better," said the sergeant. We were assured that the contents of the tube was a harmless mix of sugar and water. My thoughts were, "You gotta be shittin' me!" But it was obvious that he wasn't. None of us "leaders" had any choice, so we all did it some by jamming the needle quickly into their leg and others by slowly pushing the needle farther and farther into leg. Afterwards, all agreed that quicker was better.

At the conclusion of ROTC Summer Camp we all headed home to prepare for what we hoped was going to be our last year of college. There was still a little bit of summer left but this late in the summer all the choice jobs for college kids were taken. I settled for a job at a car wash and all I could think about the rest of the summer was spit-shined Corcoran Jump Boots, the Airborne Glider Patch on the overseas cap and the beautiful red, white and blue patch of the 82nd Airborne Division. Even though the Airborne troops seemed to consider us future officers as "college pussies," I still admired the division and the Airborne corps. How do I know they felt we were college pussies? Near the end of summer camp, we all boarded deuce-and-a-half trucks to observe an 82d Airborne Division Pass-in-Review. As we motored down the division main road, passing Airborne troopers marching in formation to the parade field, several of them yelled out, "College pussies!"

Right at the beginning of my senior year, I began flight training at VPI's own airstrip. I figured the airstrip was necessary, perhaps to fly in potential scholarship athletes for a visit, but it was also very convenient to use to introduce senior ROTC cadets who had requested flight duty with the Army or Air Force to the basics of flying. My first flight in a canvas bodied two-seater would also be my first ride in any airplane of any kind in my whole life. It was a disappointment. I thought I would be thrilled to be up in the sky peering down at the earth but I found it no more exciting than the real tame roller coaster at the local amusement park.

Also, the instructor sitting behind me was constantly yelling instructions and offering unkind comments about my ability to follow them. The first several lessons had to do with stalls— jerking back on the stick and bringing the nose of the aircraft up until it almost stalled, and then the plane would break to the right or left. Quite frankly, I found flight training boring and the guy sitting behind me was a complete jerk. I rethought my initial request for TC/Aviation and realized that what I really wanted was to be a paratroop officer in the 82nd Airborne Division. I completed the paperwork to change my branch selection and shortly after my first unassisted take off, I was removed from the flight program and re-designated as detailed to the Infantry. On June 9, 1963 I both graduated from college and received my commission as a second lieutenant. Since I elected not to take leave prior to reporting Fort Bragg and the 82nd, my report date was set for June 13, 1963.

Four

In the Army Now

A NEW SECOND LIEUTENANT (2LT, A.K.A. "BUTTER BAR") is close to the lowest form of life there is. Not only the do the troops dislike them but also officers above that lowly rank don't seem to care for them. To give everyone further reason to dislike me, I reported to the Headquarters of the 505th Parachute Infantry Regiment (PIR) in an incorrect uniform. Actually, it would have been correct in almost any other unit in the Army, but not the airborne. I wore the Class A tropical worsted uniform, shirt, tie and blouse, with the flying saucer hat and low quarter shoes. I thought it would be presumptuous of me to wear the overseas cap with the glider patch and the jump boots without having earned them. Regardless of what I thought, it was clear to me I offended one of the famous airborne units that jumped into France on D-Day. I was told by a senior NCO at battle group headquarters to take a couple of days to acquire the proper fatigue uniforms with properly affixed patches and insignia and then return. I didn't do that part right either. I went to the Post Exchange (PX), bought several sets new fatigues, some olive drab (OD) underwear, Corcoran jump boots and a fatigue cap and then went to the post tailor shop, which was also the cleaners, to have nametags made and everything sown on to my uniforms. There the lady asked me, "You want everything laundered, right?" To which I replied, "Of course not. Everything's brand new." Big mistake!

Every day in the world famous 82nd Airborne Division troopers had to "break starch." Uniforms had to be so starched that they could practically stand up by themselves. Breaking starch meant forcing your arms and legs into the sleeves and trousers of a freshly laundered uniform. Reporting in fluff dried clothing was almost as bad as wearing a saucer hat and low quarter shoes. So I was given a couple of more days to get it right and told to come back, although I sensed they wouldn't care if I never came back.

Later I heard about another new 2LT who made a bigger impression on his unit than I had. This lieutenant reported to his headquarters while only the command sergeant major was present in the building. This command sergeant major had actually jumped into combat on D-Day and he was entitled to wear the 82nd patch on his right shoulder indicating to all that he had served in combat with the division. The patch on the left shoulder merely shows that the wearer is currently assigned to the division. This other new lieutenant, observing the division patch on each of the sergeant major's shoulders, also went to the tailor shop and had the 82nd Airborne Division patch sewn on his right shoulder as well as on his left thinking that was the way it was supposed to be. I didn't witness the crap he caught for this unforgivable offense but I'm sure he will never forget it.

However, I wasn't through catching it myself. When I finally reported to my assigned unit, B Company of the 1st Airborne Battle Group, 505th PIR, my new commanding officer, Captain Reitz, asked, "When did you finish Officer Basic?"

"I haven't been yet, sir," I replied. To which he remarked, "And I see you aren't Airborne yet, so what the hell am I supposed to do with you?" I didn't reply. Then he said, "You're going to the 2d Platoon. Get with your platoon sergeant and do whatever he tells you to do."

My platoon sergeant was an O.K guy. I'm sure he wondered what he did to deserve me but, like he probably did many times before, he took me under his wing and began to teach me how to be a troop leader. While I was learning from my mentor, someone in Battle Group headquarters had gotten me scheduled for jump school at Fort Benning to begin in a week. This couldn't happen quickly enough for me because every morning as I got out of my car in the unit parking lot and walked toward B Company, shouts of "Here comes a fucking leg" rained down on me from the barracks windows above. A leg is, of course, anyone who is not a paratrooper.

On and off throughout my early break-in period, someone found an opportunity to have fun at my expense. On the first battalion jump since I joined the company, I boarded the old flying boxcar, a C-119, with my platoon. I was strapped into an Air Force parachute and showed how to pull the ripcord—"In case of emergency ONLY," I was cautioned. Once we were at jump altitude, I got out of my seat and bravely walked to one of the two open side doors of the plane. After firmly grabbing onto the interior structure, I leaned out with the wind in my face and looked at the ground about eight hundred feet below me. As I did so, I felt the firm hand of the jumpmaster grabbing the straps of the chute which passed between my legs, in the extreme vicinity of my butt, ensuring that I wouldn't fall out. My effort to show the troops I wasn't a chicken had been extremely diluted. If I thought that was bad, what happened next was true humiliation. Above the noise of aircraft engines, a staff sergeant yelled, "Hey, LT ("LT" being the universally accepted nickname for any lieutenant), the pilot wants to talk to you," and handed me a funnel shaped object connected to the wall of the plane by a flexible, metal tube. I took the funnel shaped object and said into it, "Lieutenant Colavita to pilot..." Then I noticed the whole plane was in stitches and a real platoon leader on the plane explained to me, "This funnel thing is called a relief tube. It is used by anyone on the plane who can't hold it any longer to piss into." Second lieutenants had to develop a really thick skin in order to survive eighteen months at this rank.

Finally, a rough week passed and it was time to load up my '63 Chevy, a graduation present, and head to Fort Benning, Georgia, and parachute training. Fort Benning was and still is the "Home of the Infantry," with its inspiring motto "Follow Me." When I got to Benning and settled into the officer student barracks, I met a bunch of new lieutenants who had reported to their Airborne units, both the 101st Airborne and the 82d Airborne Divisions, who had not yet been to the Basic Officer Course nor Airborne School, just like me. We compared notes on our sad experiences trying to seamlessly blend in with our new units, and it was clear we all were having a hard time fitting in. We quickly made friendships that would last as long as our careers.

Jump school was physically demanding but I was in great shape having completed the track and field season at VPI only a few weeks earlier. First off, we were given a rigorous PT test to see who was fit enough to begin the three week Airborne course. Most of us were. Those who were not would be given a week of hard PT and then be tested again.

I was among the larger group who went right into the jump course. The three weeks of jump school were Ground Week, Tower Week and Jump Week.

Ground Week: This is where you learn how to perform a satisfactory Parachute Landing Fall (PLF). The PLF is critical because almost all injuries to jumpers occur on contact with the ground. We are taught to touch down on the balls of the feet with legs together, knees bent and then commence to lean to one side or the other so the next thing to contact the ground is the side of the lower leg, then the thigh and buttocks, then, as you keep rolling, the back. The point is to spread out your contact with the ground all one side of the body. The biggest decision the jumper must make is which way to roll, and whichever way the jumper is leaning in relation to the ground when the feet make contact should make this decision pretty easy. Also in Ground Week, students meet the Swing Landing Trainer, a medieval torture device nicknamed "suspended agony." This device is a parachute harness suspended from the training shed ceiling by four parachute risers. Your feet are off the ground and your dead weight in the harness places extreme downward pressure on the family jewels, ergo, "suspended agony." But the object of the drill is to teach the jumper how to literally climb up the risers with his hands in order to steer the chute. A lot of time during Ground Week is devoted to mastering a proper PLF.

Tower Week: During this week candidates practice exiting a mock airplane door thirty-four feet above the ground while wearing a parachute harness. This harness is attached to pulleys riding on an overhead cable. After exiting the tower, when all the slack is taken up in your risers, the cable will give slightly simulating the opening of an actual parachute canopy. Then you ride this cable to the end of the line where another cable strung perpendicular abruptly stops you. Once so stopped, you swing forward and backward until some of your fellow Airborne candidates, standing on a berm at the end of the cable ride, catch you and unhook you from the pulley. Jumpers finishing the cable ride then switch places with the guys doing the catching and they will catch the next jumpers. Students repeat this cycle until each jumper has satisfied the instructors of their proficiency in obtaining a good door position. The thirty-four foot tower is tall enough that someone with a fear of heights might hesitate and realize jumping from planes may not be for him. The simulated chute opening in a thirty-four foot tower jump is actually much rougher than the real thing, and very black and blue bruises on each student's shoulders clearly identifies them as participants in Tower Week. But that's not the end of the week. There are three, 250 foot towers in the airborne training area.

One tower is like a Coney Island amusement ride in that those descending from this tower are sitting on a bench with a canopy overhead, which is raised and lowered by attached cables. There is no real free fall involved with this tower. It is usually reserved for distinguished visitors who are given a taste of parachute training. The other two towers are designed to lift the jumper up by a single cable attached to the center of a fully opened canopy. The canopy is attached to a metal ring by clips which break away from the ring when the tower operator causes the canopy to separate from the cable. The jumper then descends 250 feet just as he would after jumping from an airplane at 1000 feet. At the end of this descent the student will demonstrate a satisfactory parachute landing or become either injured or embarrassed.

Jump Week: This is where all the training comes together and troopers put on real parachutes and board real aircraft such as the C-119, the C-123, C-124 or the C-130, which is the only one of these airplanes still in military use today. As an officer I felt it was my duty to place myself at the head of a stick of jumpers in order to be the first one out the door on my side of the plane. Throughout jump school it was stressed that everyone had to have a good "door position" to ensure the chute opens properly. This entails standing in the door in a semi crouch, slapping the outside skin of the plane and then hurling yourself out the door, head down and legs tightly together. This, as opposed to timidly stepping out of the plane, which could interfere with the deployment of your canopy and result in a really bad trip to the ground. So, when I got the green light, I did what I was taught. I slapped the sides of the old C-119 and threw myself out of the plane. I counted, one thousand one, one thousand two, one thousand three, one thousand four and right on time I felt my chute open and my drop significantly slowed as my canopy filled with air. As we were taught, I looked up to check my canopy and quickly looked down again. Something was wrong.

I had a malfunction known as a Mae West. This is when a shroud line crosses over the canopy and instead of getting a fully opened chute, the shroud line crimps the canopy in or near the center, and instead of one nice round canopy, you have two smaller ones looking similar to a woman's brassier. Hence the name "Mae West," a generously endowed film actress of my parents' generation. The danger here is, if one of those canopies is smaller than the other, air rushing into the larger one can cause the nylon shroud line to be pushed over the smaller one and this rapid nylon-on-nylon movement could cause the canopy to burn up leaving no canopy at all.

I looked around. I was not descending any faster than anyone else but I still faced the possibility of watching my canopy burn up. So I did as we were instructed to do, although I never dreamed I'd be in this position. Maybe that's why I didn't pay that much attention to the class on deploying the reserve. I pulled the handle on my reserve parachute pack but I failed to grab the white reserve chute in order to shake it out and help it fill with air. The slower the descent, the harder it is to get the reserve chute to catch the air. It dropped straight down below my spit shined Corcoran jump boots and began wrapping itself around my body so I could no longer see anything except white parachute fabric. I began fighting with the canopy hoping to see where I was in relation to the ground when I hear, "Relax your knees," being yelled by a megaphone-amplified voice. *I must be close to the ground*, I thought, and as I did as the voice commanded, I promptly slammed ass first into the unyielding turf of our Drop Zone (DZ) in Alabama. It knocked the wind out of me but I was still conscious and wondering what all I broke. Other jumpers and staff got me out of the tangled two canopied mess and a military ambulance was already on the scene. I was checked out on the ground, still not sure what condition I was in, and then driven off the DZ in the ambulance. By the time we got to the sidelines, I had recovered my breath and found that nothing was broken. The medics ensured I was not in need of further treatment and I was able to board one of the vehicles taking us back to Fort Benning.

That night I had Technicolor dreams of me splattered all over Alabama and when I awoke the next morning, everything I owned was sore and stiff. I was able to move but with great pain, and I was further pained when the Airborne instructors, this second day of Jump Week, used me as an example of a poor door position. I knew I had a good position but dared not say a thing. Later on that second day's flight to the DZ, I positioned myself so that I was the last member of a stick and I would be the last one to go out the door on my side of the plane. In all honesty, I didn't know whether or not I was going to jump until I found myself outside the plane staring up at a perfectly formed canopy.

The final three jumps of Airborne school were uneventful. I'll never forget and never ceased to be amazed at how it feels after the planes pass by, you are out the door and the planes have moved on and you find yourself several hundred feet in the air in absolute peace and quiet. The planes are too far away to hear their engine noise, and you are too high up to hear any sounds from the ground. Then, thinking about jumping in combat, I figured there is really no way Fort Benning can safely allow you to experience what it feels like to be helplessly hanging in the air while people on the ground are shooting at you and trying for all they are worth to kill you. Only a real combat jump can show a jumper what that's like.

****

Airborne School ended and the graduation ceremony was a nice event. We said goodbye to new friends, headed to our rooms to collect our packed bags and then headed back to our duty stations, mostly Fort Bragg and the 82nd and Fort Campbell, Kentucky, and the 101st.

Not everyone who graduated from jump school was going back to an Airborne unit. A large number of students were brand new soldiers who requested Airborne training and have yet to be assigned to a unit. Others are already assigned to non-airborne units but who have asked for parachute training so they are qualified to request a transfer to the airborne. Others, mostly newly commissioned officers, simply wanted to wear the parachutist wings on their uniforms and had no intention of ever jumping out of a perfectly good plane again. The Airborne School drew a distinction between what they considered a parachutist and a paratrooper. As I drove back to Fort Bragg and the 505th, I enjoyed the thought of never having to hear "Fucking leg" yelled at me again from the barracks. Except, you are not really considered Airborne until you make what is called your "cherry jump." That is the name for your first jump after graduating from Airborne School.

Someone in operations had scheduled me soon after my return from Benning to perform my cherry jump and become a real paratrooper. This was to be a jump from a Huey helicopter, a UH-1B, over Sicily Drop Zone. As jumps go, it would be hard to find an easier jump. There would be no gathering at the airfield where we would sit on the tarmac forever, followed by a forty-five minute flight simulating flying into combat, as well as accumulating flying time for the USAF Reserve pilots. Instead, the four other jumpers and I went to the Army airfield, got on a waiting chopper, took off, flew a few short minutes until we were over the drop zone at jump altitude, then, one at a time, we hung our legs out the doors, stepped onto the chopper skids and then stepped off into space. There was no violent prop blast and a relatively easy opening of the chute followed by a gentle descent and landing not far from the vehicle waiting to take us back to the unit area.

The next several weeks involved field training exercises, including several jumps, as well as standing Division Ready Force (DRF) and Initial Ready Force (IRF) where we literally surrounded the battalion area with barbwire, with all hands on deck. Our combat gear was packed and we were prepared to go anywhere in the world on a moment's notice. In August, it was time to go back to Fort Benning to attend the Infantry Officers Basic Course (IOBC). Here we would meet our West Point counterparts for the first time. They were easy to identify. They had just finished sixty days of leave and were wearing the same fluff dried fatigues some of us ROTC types had until we got educated. We, on the other hand, were wearing rigidly starched fatigues with all patches and insignia properly displayed, a number of us with jump wings. This would be an interesting situation where each of the two groups of new lieutenants felt superior to the other: ROTC because we had some experience and looked better in our uniforms, and the USMA because they had graduated from the premier producer of career Army officers.

Throughout the twelve week course, the West Pointers and ROTC guys tried to hang with their own but the IOBC staff and faculty had ways of mixing us up. Mixing the two groups together was actually a good idea since down the road we would both work together for the good of the Army and the soldiers we commanded.

Following Infantry Basic, most of us would go on to Ranger School, a nine week course designed to break you down and rebuild you into a fighting machine. I don't remember the drop-out/flunk-out rate but suffice it to say, not everyone makes it through to graduation. The Ranger School Cadre really knew how to mix the West Point and ROTC groups. On the first day in the Fort Benning phase, we were instructed to pick a Ranger Buddy. Ranger Buddies are required to watch each other's backs. On cold nights outdoors when only another person's body heat can keep you warm, Ranger Buddies were taught to roll up together in a rubber poncho. This was a difficult concept for most of us, but freezing on a cold fall night caused everyone to try the two-man poncho thing and it worked.

Ranger Buddies would role play the rescued and the rescuer in exercises carrying each other out of danger and, last but not least, Ranger Buddies would square off against each other in hand-to-hand combat in the pit. Here was a chance to mess with your Ranger Buddy (until you realized he could do the same thing to you), as in, "Sergeant, I don't think I understood that throw with the chop to the neck. Can I see it again?" And, of course, the sergeant demonstrated it again, on your Ranger Buddy.

On the first day of Ranger training, when we were first told to pick a Ranger Buddy, all the West Point guys chose a West Pointer and the ROTC guys picked another ROTC guy. As soon as the picking was done, the cadre advised, "Now we're going to do it again and each West Point trainee will pick an ROTC Ranger Buddy and visa versa." And we did and it worked out fine.

Ranger School was too tough for anyone to be concerned with where one graduated from college or the source of one's commission. Ranger School primarily stressed patrolling, which involved small unit tactics where every man had a job to do and everyone worked together to accomplish the mission. The Ranger instructors, or lane graders, were usually senior NCOs and they were professional and extremely competent. Here was a situation where the primarily enlisted staff could, if they had a mind to, really screw with a bunch of junior officers.

Our class, designated as Ranger Class 4-63, was composed entirely of officers. The Ranger School is not strictly a school for officers but every year following West Point and ROTC graduations and commissioning, a couple of all-officer classes is not unusual. The Fort Benning phase was very busy and no one had time to think about anything except not screwing up. Ranger School was known for not tolerating stupidity or laziness or incompetence. The school, I believe, was proud of its record of candidates quitting or washing out.

Before we knew it, the weather turned colder and we were about to move to the Mountain Phase of training at a camp in the mountains of Delonega, Georgia. In the mountain camp, we were assigned bunks in small cabins where our stuff remained while we learned repelling and patrolling in the mountains. We had wood burning stoves in each hooch that barely kept us warm. At least we didn't have to get cozy again in a poncho with another guy! For those who had to get up in the middle of the night to pee, the correct way was to quietly exit the hooch and walk a few yards to the latrine. The incorrect way was to exit the hooch, stand on the wooden steps and attempt to pee as far away from the steps as possible. All night long you would hear from subsequent pissers, "Aw shit!" as they stepped in what the guys before them did.

****

I got two chances at leading a patrol in the mountains and I passed one and failed the other. I really don't think the failure was fair, I didn't think so then and I don't think so now. We were on the way back from accomplishing our fictitious mission. Three or four other guys were assigned the duty as patrol leader up to that point and, just as we were to return to "friendly lines," I got tapped with the patrol leader's job. This might be only a land navigation drill back to the same point where we departed friendly lines, or more than that if the cadre had some surprises for us, like an ambush. Turns out there was no ambush and I brought the patrol back to the same point where we began our patrol.

The lane grader, an NCO older and more grizzled than most, began to question me as to how I knew I had returned the patrol to the right place. I did the best I could do to convince him that I knew I was correct. But, he continued, "What if I tell you, Ranger, that you're in the wrong goddam place even though you think you're right?" I started to have doubts.

"Sergeant, if you tell me I'm in the wrong place I guess I'm in the wrong place."

"So you're not so sure anymore, huh?"

"No sergeant, I'm not so sure anymore."

"Well you are in the correct place but since you're not so sure anymore, you just flunked this patrol!"

I was crushed. We're only half way through school with the entire Florida swamp phase left to go and I was only fifty-fifty for patrols. There was no discussion nor any appeal. From this point on I had better be very careful.

Another opportunity arose that could have gotten me in terminal trouble except that half the class had committed the same crime. On

November 22, 1963, we were in formation being inspected for the final patrol in the mountain phase. The inspection included being shaken down for candy or other contraband we might have bought at the camp PX and squirreled away to nibble on while on patrol. Suddenly, another officer from the cadre rushed up and whispered something in our inspector's ear. Our inspector then turned towards us with a shocked look on his face and said, "Gentlemen, we have a new President of the United States." My first thought was, "Have we been out in the boondocks that damn long?" But then our inspector continued, "President Kennedy has been assassinated in Dallas, Texas." Collectively, we all thought. "Yeah, right." I know I thought that, and was pretty sure everyone else thought that this assassination of the president was part of the patrol scenario, particularly since our preparation for the patrol continued. We were told we were moving from the inspection stage to the rehearsal stage. Then, suddenly everything was called off. We were told to stow our gear in our hooches and report immediately to the camp briefing building.

This we all did and that's where we learned about Lee Harvey Oswald and the swearing in of President Lyndon B. Johnson. We watched the TV in stunned silence. After we watched all the news and realized for sure we did have a new President of the United States, half of us were further stunned when an announcement was made that there would be a memorial formation the next day at 0700 in the main street of the camp and the uniform would be Class A green uniforms. The reason half of us were stunned was because that was approximately how many of us disregarded the requirement to bring a Class A uniform with us. The rationale for requiring a Class A uniform was so that those who wanted to could attend Sunday church services at nearby community churches. Like me, I assumed those of us who did not bring the uniforms didn't want to go to church.

The next day the formation was held as ordered, except for the mix of dress and field uniforms. There were too many of us without the dress uniform, both West Point and ROTC, that a major ass chewing was about all they could do without setting a new record for washed out Ranger candidates.

****

The swamp phase of Ranger School was located at Eglin Air Force Base in the Florida panhandle. The good news for us was that in December the alligators and other denizens were hibernating or just moving slowly. The bad news was, the swamp water was quite high and freezing cold. Patrolling in the swamp was no fun at all. We all had reflectorized material sewn on the backs of our caps. Most of these were parallel strips looking like captains bars, but weak swimmer's strips were in the form of a "T" so they could be more easily identified. Over the years, Ranger candidates have drowned in the swamp phase of Ranger School and we were each required to keep a sharp eye on the Ranger in front of us.

I received a passing grade on my only swamp phase patrol and it was clear at that point that I would be getting my Ranger Tab. Two friends of mine, a West Point graduate and, would you believe, a Naval Academy graduate who for some reason selected the Army to serve in, did not receive the tab.

Soon we would be headed back to our units having graduated from Airborne, Infantry Officer Basic and Ranger Schools. Except for not having any real experience in the job, we were now fully qualified to function as Infantry platoon leaders.

The Ranger School cadre did strike a final blow that I'm sure gave them some satisfaction. Today, if one were to go to the Fort Benning website and click on "Ranger School," then on "Class Pictures," then go to the FY 1963 class pictures and click on

Class 4-63, one would see that our class is the only class in the entire history of the U. S. Army Ranger School wearing the Class A green uniforms in our graduation picture. Every other class is wearing the field uniform. I guess they just didn't want us to forget.

We graduated with our new Ranger Tabs in December just before Christmas. We all planned to go home on leave for the holidays and then return to our units. The class behind us, also an all-officer West Point/ROTC bunch, also went home for Christmas but had to report back to the Eglin AFB Swamp Phase after the holidays. Tough break!

The first six months of what I planned to be at least a twenty-year career were drawing to a close. A lot had happened in those six months. At the beginning of the next six months I had two significant things happen, one was very good and the other sucked.

First, the good one. The division operated its own Jump Master Course at Fort Bragg. This was a desirable qualification to have and it was an absolute necessity for earning senior or master jump wings. A second lieutenant, however, had no chance in hell of getting into the Jump Master Course. Then, out of the blue, B Company threw me into a slot in the school replacing our company executive officer (XO) who had a family emergency and had to cancel. I graduated from the course in February 1964 and subsequently served as Jump Master on several company drops.

The bad thing happened in the spring. The Army was still very much into inter and intra service sports. One of those sports was track and field. One of my roommates (five of us from the Ranger School assigned to the 82nd rented a nice house just off post) mentioned to someone that I had been a scholarship runner at VPI. This got back to the Battle Group Executive Officer,

Colonel Murphy. Everybody was afraid of Colonel Murphy so I
was quaking in my boots when I was summoned to his office.
"Lieutenant, I understand you were a scholarship track runner
at Virginia Tech," he said. "Quarter mile and mile relay were
your specialties, right?"
"Yes, sir."
"Well, effective immediately you are reassigned to the division
track team. You will report to the team coach. They know you're
coming and you will be at the post stadium tomorrow at 0700."
"But sir," said I, "I really would prefer to stay a platoon leader.
Besides, I've been having some sinus trouble and I'm having
difficulty breathing through my nose which will interfere with
my running," I said, pulling that excuse right out of my ass.
"Fuck your nose," replied the colonel. "Be at the stadium
tomorrow."
So at 0700 the next day, appropriately dressed in sweats and
running shoes, I reported to the track coach who held the rank of
specialist fifth class. Early on, they arranged for a quarter mile
run off between myself and a wiry black enlisted trooper who
was currently the fastest man in the quarter mile. I gave some
thought to throwing the race but since it took four men to do the
mile relay, I'd still be on the team. So I beat him. So many of the
onlookers were surprised and shocked. I was not a happy camper
though. I wasn't doing a soldier's job and instead of throwing a
few drinks back in the evening with the boys at the 82d Officer's
Club, I was again an athlete in training.
After about a week of going to track practice instead of B
Company, I arrived at the practice track and was met by the
assistant coach. He said, "Coach has been arrested and we need
to go to the Provost Marshal's Office and see what we can do for
him." I guess I was part of "we" because I was the only officer
on the team. When we got to the PMO and I heard the charge

was child molesting, I told the arresting CID agents, "I really don't even know this guy," and left. Now the question was, what about the track team? With a very clear directive, "Fuck your nose," Colonel Murphy declared that I was a runner now and not a platoon leader. But, the times they were a changing. The U. S. Army was in the process of doing a thorough reorganization. The battle groups were turning back into brigades consisting of two to five battalions. The 505th PIR was about to become the first and second battalions of the 505th. Along with that, the Vietnam conflict was beginning to get everybody's attention and senior officers and NCOs who saw combat in WW II or Korea were retiring by the boatload. And finally, swept up in everything else going on, all Army sports were immediately deemphasized to the point that all athletes were being returned to their units as soldiers. Somewhere in the reorganization, Colonel Murphy got lost and I returned to B Company, 1st Battalion of the 505th. Parachute Infantry.

If I had any thoughts of putting my platoon leader hat on and being the leader of my forty-some troops, I soon realized that wasn't going to happen. Right on the heels of the division reorganization, the Army was facing spring and the arrival of a new crop of second lieutenants, the Class of 1964. Existing platoon leaders had to vacate those positions and become battalion motor officers, mess officers and staff assistants at battalion or even brigade level. Under the new reorganization, the Battalion Communications Officer was an Infantry officer trained in communications. I was designated to be that person.

A real Signal Corps officer would be found at brigade level, but I was off again to Fort Benning to attend the Infantry School Communications Officer Course. It was only a couple of weeks where I and several other lucky Infantry lieutenants learned the capabilities and limitations of Army radios and field telephones. We also had a brief course in telephone pole climbing.

I'm sorry, but my head wasn't into radios and telephones. My mind was racing ahead six months at which time I should be promoted to first lieutenant and be eligible to request a transfer to the U. S. Army Military Assistance Command, Vietnam (MACV). The advisory effort was still all the American military was doing in Vietnam at that time and I needed to be a part of the action. Even though Vietnam was getting known as a dirty little war full of booby traps, ambushes and an invisible enemy, everyone still felt that we would whip the Viet Cong in short order.

Of the five lieutenants living together, I was determined to be the first one to get to Vietnam. Fortunately, as communications officer, I had two great NCOs—a sergeant first class and a staff sergeant—who knew commo, and they propped me up in this position. The only thing I took away from my six months as the battalion communications guy was that while we were sitting high on a mountain top with a couple of three-quarter ton trucks loaded with radio components and a sky high RC 292 coaxial antenna that we could make taller by putting the mast head up in a tree (thank goodness for the telephone pole climbing course), we still couldn't communicate with our troops at the bottom of the hill. But then Smokey the Park Ranger would drive up in his 4WD pickup with a little dashboard mounted Motorola, and he could talk with fellow Rangers in the next county.

When I returned from Benning and the Commo Course, the 1/505 had a new commander, Lieutenant Colonel (LTC) Calvert P. Benedict. He had replaced the previous commander, LTC Elbert E. Legg (yes, you heard that right). LTC Benedict was tall, fit and wore the Master Parachute wings and, on his dress uniform, he wore a Distinguished Service Cross, a combat award second only to the Medal Of Honor. I could sense in my few contacts with him that he wasn't impressed with me as a go-getter. Under other circumstances, I would have loved to impress this impressive officer but my efforts now were concentrated on getting to Vietnam.

December 1964 came and the promotion fairy touched my roommates and I and we became first lieutenants (1LT). On the sly, I had visited the battalion Personnel Office and completed my request for a transfer to MACV. Approval came quickly but not exactly as I expected it. I was going to be assigned to MACV but first I had to attend the Military Assistance Training Advisor (MATA) Course located in the Special Forces portion of Fort Bragg for three weeks. Then I would travel to Monterey, California, where I would study the Vietnamese language for eight weeks at the Defense Language Institute (DLI). Almost three months of training before I would see Vietnam. I was disappointed, but still felt sure I would be in combat before my roommates.

Late the night after my first day in the MATA Course, the house phone rang as it had done so many times during our almost two years in that house. I stifled my reaction to answer the phone. I reminded myself, "You're not in the 82nd any more so that call is not for you." I heard one of my roommates get the call. Minutes later I heard the sound of boots in a hurry followed by the sounds of the front door opening and closing and a then car starting and leaving. I heard the phone, the boots, the door and the car three more times that night. The next morning I woke up in the house alone. I had no idea where everyone went.

On my lunch hour from MATA training, I went to the little cleaners off post that we all used for our uniforms. While I was picking up my starched fatigues, Hilda, the proprietor, asked, "Why didn't you go off to the Dominican Republic like all them other boys?" It turns out that my roommates not only got into combat before me, they also were awarded the coveted Combat Infantryman's Badge before me. So much for being slick.

The first elements of the 82nd to enter the "DomRep," as it became known, indeed saw combat and took casualties. Had I not been in such a hurry to see combat, I actually would have seen it sooner. As if to pour salt in a wound, one of my roommates actually got to Vietnam before me, while I was still in the Vietnamese language course, and began serving as an advisor to a Vietnamese Ranger battalion.

Five

The Republic of Vietnam
Airborne Brigade

I F YOU WERE AIRBORNE QUALIFIED AND SENT TO Vietnam as an advisor, the Republic of Vietnam (RVN) Airborne Brigade Advisory Detachment was an assignment to die for. And since the establishment of the Airborne Advisory Team 162 in the 1950s under the U. S. Military Assistance Advisory Group (MAAG), later known as the Military Assistance Command, Vietnam (MACV), many men who got that assignment did die.

The original Vietnamese Airborne Brigade, grown to division size by December 1965, partnered with Team 162 until February 1973. While I served with the brigade, beginning in the summer of 1965, I gave the enemy many opportunities to kill me and they almost succeeded.

I was assigned as the assistant battalion advisor to the 5th Battalion. My radio call sign was Red Hat 5 Alpha. The senior battalion advisor, Captain Gerald "Tex" Sewell, was Red Hat 5 and the team NCO, Sergeant First Class John Milender, was Red Hat 5 Bravo. SFC Milender and I arrived in-country at the same time and were both new to the Airborne Advisory Detachment. The Red Hat call sign came from the distinctive red berets worn by the RVN Airborne. The 5th Battalion headquarters was located in a walled compound just off Highway 1, about midway between Bien Hoa and Saigon. Our three man team was billeted at the Vietnamese Armor School compound at Thu Duc about half-way between battalion headquarters and Saigon. Most of the rest of the U.S. Airborne advisors, as well as the advisory team headquarters staff, lived in a well-appointed and secured mansion in Saigon called the Manor. One battalion, the 7th, was remotely located from Saigon.

I may have missed out on the trip to the Dominican Republic with my 82nd roommates but I seriously lucked out getting this assignment with the RVN Airborne Advisors. While in the Vietnamese language course at Monterey, I heard a number of my fellow students talking about this detachment and what they were going to do to try to get assigned to it. As a matter of fact, if I hadn't heard them talk about it, I wouldn't have even known about the possibility of an Airborne assignment. I heard guys say they were going to contact Infantry Branch and make a case to get assigned to the Airborne. I heard guys say they were going to contact a particular general officer and try to his help getting an Airborne assignment. One guy was even going to call his congressman and ask for his help getting an Airborne job. For my part, after hearing all of this, I wrote a short note to a captain I had known in the 505th asking if he might be able to help me get assigned to the Airborne Brigade. The only reason I even knew this captain was an advisor with the RVN Airborne Brigade was because he was also mentioned in conversation; but, I guess, no one thought a captain could be much help getting a coveted Airborne job. (Now, before you conclude that I am some kind of weasel listening in on private conversations, these were very loud discussions by guys getting sloshed at the officers' club bar after class and I was among them.)

I had met Captain Chuck Toftoy when we were both in 505th at Fort Bragg. In these loud conversations, I learned that he was the senior battalion advisor to the 7th Battalion of the Airborne Brigade. I already knew the MACV APO (Army Post Office) address since it was on all of our orders. So while others tried to talk to Infantry Branch, or to some general officer or their congressman, I simply sent my Airborne acquaintance a note asking about the possibility of getting an Airborne job, and I got a note back from him telling me that I would be picked up by someone from the Team after my last MACV orientation class in Saigon. I didn't know if this would really happen or not, but it did. Many lieutenants and captains in the orientation class with me looked at me with envy as I climbed aboard the jeep with the Airborne Brigade markings. I never saw Chuck Toftoy to thank him for getting me this assignment. His battalion was the one located northeast of Saigon along the coast at Vung Tau and our paths never crossed again.

****

In what I thought would be my first taste of combat, we were tasked with going to the rescue of a Special Forces camp in the central highlands at a place called Duc Co, very near the border with Cambodia. We flew up north on C-123s and then on to the camp by helicopters. It was not a hot LZ when we landed. Reinforcements sent ahead of the 5th battalion, as well as local Montagnard mountain tribesmen, called "Yards" for short, trained by the Special Forces, had successfully driven the enemy off. As the chopper I was on dropped down to land on the camp airstrip, the rotor wash blew away the ponchos covering the dead friendlies and I would recall that scene years later as I watched the Vietnam war movie, "Platoon." So, there was no fighting left to do. We camped along the airstrip overnight and as I was rolling up my gear the next morning, a tall American major in the Airborne uniform walking by said, "Shave lieutenant, ASAP." Turns out it was the task force senior advisor Major Norman Schwarzkopf. I shaved ASAP.

With no fighting left to do and time to kill while our return travel plans were being made, the American Airborne advisors spent the morning as the guests of the Yards. It should be noted that the ethnic Vietnamese were not fond of the mountain dwelling Montagnards and the feeling was mutual, so the RVN officers did not join us. The Yards offered us food and some native-brewed alcoholic drink. I learned in my advisor training at Fort Bragg that we should not refuse what was offered to us by our native hosts. I ate and drank, and shortly thereafter, my stomach was in dire straits.

I felt it would be best if I went into the Special Forces camp and found the latrine, which I did. The latrine was a wooden structure with a roof, side and rear walls and a front that was screened from about the neck up of those sitting on the crapper bench inside. The bench was a three holer with the holes directly above cut down fifty-five gallon drums, which could be pulled out from the rear, the contents of which would be doused with aviation fuel and then burned by the unlucky souls who drew this duty. I was the only occupant of the latrine but shortly I was addressed by a Green Beret captain standing out front and speaking to me through the screen. "Lieutenant," he said, "I am ordering you out of the latrine and outside the wire, ASAP. This facility is reserved for the Special Forces soldiers assigned to this camp." Unlike Major Schwarzkopf, this asshole deserved no response. With my stomach still gurgling, I pulled up my pants and exited the latrine and the camp under the steely glare of the captain. All these many years later, I am still pissed off about suffering this indignity at the hands of another American soldier.

****

Although I saw no combat on that operation, I learned that the Red Hat officers and NCOs fought hard when it was time, and they also played hard when it was time. And though the 5th Battalion advisors did not have rooms at the Manor, it was understood by those who did that, when they were in the field, their rooms and the amenities of the Manor were to be used by the guys who were housed elsewhere when they came to Saigon.

While staying at the Manor, Captain "Tex" Sewell asked me to go with him to downtown To Do (Freedom) Street to visit the detachment's favorite watering hole, The King Bar. Apparently, my captain was a favorite of the bar girls. It seems, before my time, a drunk soldier got angry for some reason and threw a glass ashtray which struck a circulating ceiling fan and shattered, showering everyone with broken glass. While less drunk soldiers threw the really drunk one out, Tex sprang into action using his handkerchief to stop the bleeding of a bar girl who took a piece of glass to her forehead. From that point forward, this appreciative girl would be Tex's girl whenever he was in town.

On my first visit to the King Bar, Tex introduced me to his girl and she introduced me to her friend who would be *my* girl whenever I was in town. My girl's name was, of course, Suzy. Suzy was not only a bar girl charged with getting GIs to buy her Saigon Tea, a nonalcoholic drink that was really expensive, but she was also the singer with the house band. I was completely impressed with her version of the Connie Francis song "Frankie My Darling." In Suzy's version, the song went, "I been so ronrey since you been apart."

On a subsequent visit to Saigon, following several days in the field, Suzy purred to me, "After work you come my house, we do boom-boom, OK?" I couldn't turn down an invitation like that. As the bar was shutting down, Suzy and I left and grabbed one of the many yellow and blue Renault cabs that roamed the city and we went to her place not far from the bar. Her dwelling was some sort of a one floor row house. We walked in and I saw it was a single room with a cooking area and a bathroom area. The sleeping areas were divided by thin mosquito netting. Sitting at a table eating and drinking were an old man, an old woman and a young man who could have been Suzy's little brother or, for that matter, her son. In my best Vietnamese I said, "*Chao Ong*" to Papasan (literally "hello gentleman"), "*Chao Ba*" to Mamasan (literally "hello married woman") and "*Chao Dude*" (which was the best I could do for "hello young man").

Suzy didn't waste any time escorting me to her sleeping area behind the netting through which I could clearly see the family and they could clearly see us. Suzy stripped down and got under the sheet. I sheepishly stripped down to my underwear and also got under the sheet. If Bugs Bunny had walked in just then and asked, "What's up Doc?" I could have told him what was *not* up. I told Suzy I had a headache and she turned on her side and went to sleep. At some point, the people on the other side of the curtains retired behind their respective nets but it was too late, the damage was done.

With everyone sleeping, including Suzy, I silently got out of bed, slipped into my clothes, which were lying in a heap where I dropped them, left a few *dong* (Vietnamese dollars, really!) on the pillow, tiptoed to the closest door and exited.

I found myself standing in a dark alley with a muscular, military aged young man who was curling a homemade barbell made from a long piece of pipe with concrete weights on each end. I again said, "*Chao Ong*," wondering for an instant why the Vietnamese language didn't differentiate between greeting a shriveled up toothless old gentleman and a young muscular guerilla fighter, or whatever he was. He nodded in response to my greeting and cranked out another curl.

Thanks to Americans like the jerk who threw the ashtray in the King Bar, we were not allowed to carry weapons of any kind while off duty in Saigon. I didn't even have a nail clipper to defend myself in the event this guy was Viet Cong (VC), or Suzy's older brother. He may have been both of those things but all he did was stare at me as I carefully slid down the alley and to the street where I hailed an ever present Renault cab.

Shortly after returning to our quarters at Thu Duc, the 5th Battalion departed on a multi-force operation and I rarely returned to the King Bar afterwards. Instead, I decided that when we were out of the field and I could get to Saigon, I would go to Tan Son Nhut Airport where the Vietnamese Airborne School had plane loads of paratrooper trainees jumping daily. I had earned my Senior Parachutist Wings at the very beginning of this assignment and I decided to earn my Master Wings by the end of this tour of duty. In fact, I decided that even if I had to extend my assignment with the RVN Airborne in order to get the required amount of time on jump status and the total number of jumps I needed, I would do so in order to get my Master Wings.

****

Many of our trips to the boondocks produced no major contact with the enemy. I figured this was because, under the best of circumstances, hundreds of men tramping through the jungle would make a racket but carrying metal pots and pans and live farm animals along just about guaranteed that everyone in the jungle knew we were coming. The Vietnamese also had some squirrelly ideas which may have been designed to avoid combat. There was the time we planned for and fired hundreds of American artillery shells in front of us on our route of march because intelligence believed there was a high probability that a large concentration of enemy was at the location where the rounds were headed. After the barrage, the Vietnamese task force commander changed the route of march saying, "Now that the VC think they know where we are going, we go somewhere else." If intelligence was right, think of all the dead and wounded enemy we would never meet.

Of course, we engaged in many operations where we did have contact. On one search-and-destroy mission we were constantly sniped at and we also encountered suicide VC who popped up from spider holes within our formation and killed or wounded a few troopers before they were killed. I was new to the war and I wanted to kill VC and North Vietnamese Army (NVA) soldiers, but the RVN paratroopers I was with had been fighting the war for years. The RVN airborne had fought alongside the French in their fight with the Viet Minh from 1946 to 1954. In fact, their Airborne camouflaged uniform with the jaunty red beret and the very design of their jump wings were modeled after the French. During my time with these soldiers, I saw some of them die from wounds which should not have even been life threatening. I recall on our return trips to the 5th Battalion compound after an operation, it seemed to me that all the soldiers' wives and family were sobbing and wailing as the trucks rolled in. Then, as they saw their man had returned alive, they stopped crying. Even though we visiting Americans were full of piss and vinegar ready to kill commies for Christ, these soldiers and their families, I believed, were quite tired of war. Later, of course, I would wonder why the Vietnamese from the North weren't *that* tired.

****

If thinking about meeting a muscle bound VC in a dark alley sent a chill up my backside, I managed to do other dumb things on this tour of duty which still make me cringe today just thinking about them.

One operation sent us up north to the area of Pleiku with the task of keeping a major highway open. The VC had cut major trenches across the mountain highway interrupting supplies moving on U.S. and RVN convoys. On this operation I was traveling with the 54th Company commanded by Dai Uy (Captain) Tinh. He was the most personable of the battalion's five company commanders and also the best English speaker.

The company took a position high on a hillside where we had a good view of the section of highway we were protecting. We were too far away from the road to engage the enemy with small arms but in a great position to direct artillery or aircraft. SFC Milender was traveling with another company responsible for another section of highway, so we couldn't hang together overnight as we usually did.

I was unpacking my gear and getting ready for a night of highway watching when Captain Tinh and an entourage approached me. The captain said, "*Trung Uy*, (lieutenant) I am going down to the stream we crossed earlier to bathe. Would you care to join me?" I saw he had his toothbrush, hairbrush and toiletries with him. I, however, politely declined having gotten used to being scruffy and smelly. I watched the captain and his protectors disappear over the hill to descend a couple of hundred yards to the stream below. Then I had second thoughts. Ugly American! I didn't want my counterpart or any of his troops to think we American advisors were unclean pigs. So I gathered up my soap, razor, shaving cream, towel and pistol and started down the mountain. Imagine my unhappiness when I met Captain Tinh and his men about half way back returning to the top of the hill. Big decision. Do I turn around and go back with the captain and lose face, or continue down to the stream to what might be the last bath I ever take. I elected to go down to the stream. I'll never know if Captain Tinh left some guys behind to keep an eye on me or not. Shortly, I was standing ankle deep in the stream shaving and brushing my teeth and never feeling so alone in my life. I could have been killed by a long distance shot or surrounded by VC or NVA and had my throat cut. Or, worse yet, I could have been stuffed into a 3x3 foot bamboo cage and hauled around until I finally ended up at the Hanoi Hilton. Praying all the way back, I packed up my stuff, picked up my pistol and started back up hill. If Captain Tinh had left anyone behind to cover me I saw no trace of them on my way back. I have been thanking God every day since then that I didn't get killed or captured standing in that stream.

****

After the highway security job up north, Captain Sewell, SFC Milender and I were hanging out at our billets when we were summoned to Saigon with full combat equipment and weapon for a quickie operation in the Capital Military Region, the area around Saigon, which was itself surrounded by both III and IV Corps Tactical Zones (CTZ). We were briefed on a multi-battalion air assault we would be making from Saigon's Tan Son

Nhut Airport into the paddy lands just outside the city. Intelligence had confirmed heavy VC activity around the airport and concluded that it was going to be attacked.

Very quickly, the 5th and 6th Airborne Battalions were assembled at the airport where we loaded onto choppers and flown a relatively short distance where we were dropped off at scattered locations in the mixed grassy and rice paddy lands. Immediately, groups of black pajama clad Cong jumped up from the tall grass in front of us and began running towards a small village about two hundred yards away. I started running after a group to my front who were themselves running toward the village. I raised my rifle and began shooting at the group. Aiming was difficult because I was running as fast as I could and, you recall, I was a former track star. I fired a burst at the running pajama boys and one fell down. Then, in an admirable act of brotherly love, the Cong closest to him picked him up and continued to run, carrying the wounded guy piggyback. I grabbed the radio handset clipped to the epaulet on my right shoulder, "Red Hat 5 this is Red Hat 5A…" I got that out just as the handset was yanked out of my hand. I looked back to see my RTO standing the full distance of the stretched out handset cord from me and the rest of the company at a considerable distance behind him. I was way out in front of everyone and wisely turned and ran back to friendly forces.

As more friendly troops were lifted into the area, the Cong mostly successfully made it into the built up village. They must have already had defensive positions in the village because withering fire started coming our way. Now we were the ones with the problem because the Cong had cover and concealment and all we had were the rice paddy dikes. As freshly landed friendly troops rushed for cover, a passing U.S. advisor yelled to me, "Rocky, Suzy says 'Hi.'"

Our troops spread out in a long line facing the unfriendly village, everyone trying to get real small behind a paddy dike. Then, again the tide shifted. Vietnamese Air Force A1E Skyraider fighter bombers and U.S. helicopter gunships had lifted off from Tan Son Nhut and were immediately overhead. Now the Cong had to concern themselves with death from above as well as from their immediate front. The A1Es came in low and slow and dropped ordinance, to include napalm, directly onto the village. If there were any innocent civilians at home they were being smoked along with the VC. As the recently arrived air power took charge of the situation, the VC came up with a unique way to avoid being melted by the napalm. As the low and slow A1Es came in on a run, the VC would scamper out of the village and take their chances with our marksmanship by running in circles out in the open. After the napalm had exploded sucking the oxygen out of the air and igniting anything it stuck to, those who survived the shooting gallery would run back into the village.

As an assistant battalion advisor I had no duty in these circumstances other than to function as a rifleman. I had a radio, which only communicated with the senior advisor. It would be him and not me talking to Air Force Forward Air Controllers (FACs), helicopter gunships or artillery. So, I decided to earn my pay as a rifleman.

Our advisory detachment had recently traded the WW II weapons we were issued from our RVN battalion arms rooms for first generation M-16s. I was sorry to lose my M2 paratrooper model carbine with the folding stock and fully automatic selector switch, but I knew I had a better weapon. I had also come across some 5.56mm tracer ammunition, which I mixed in with the regular rounds in my magazines. I decided I would get at least one of the VC running around outside cover as the next A1E came in. And it was inbound.

As the plane swooped in, the black pajama gang again ran out into the open. I picked out my man and began shooting aimed single shots. As the occasional tracer round came out I could see I was all around this guy. I straightened up and repositioned myself on the paddy dike and fired some more. This time I saw a tracer round and the man's head meet and he dropped out of sight. Only then did I realize I was kneeling on the paddy dike and fully exposed from my head to my knees, but I was so pleased with my kill that, as I dropped down toward better cover, I turned to my left and then to my right to do a high five with a fellow trooper on either side of me—but no one slapped my hand.

The guys on my left and right were both dead, shot in the foreheads above the eyebrows. The little bit of themselves they exposed to the enemy fire cost them their lives. Again, God saw fit to save me despite my foolish behavior. After a while the VC began running out the back of the village towards another village and then from that village into the thick vegetation that marked the beginning of the surrounding jungle. A decision was made at some level that we would not pursue and the exercise was over. As the undead paratroopers stood up from the paddy dikes protecting them, the number who continued to lie face down in the muck was shocking.

After the fight near the airport things calmed down. There were more nature walks with a couple of hundred close friends accompanied by occasional exchanges of gunfire and mortars. I never saw many of the Cong booby traps such as punji pits or swinging tree trunks full of bamboo spikes designed to wipe out several careless trail walkers. I figured it was because both sides in this fight were crisscrossing the same terrain.

Out of the field, SFC Milender and I continued to rule the pool table at Thu Duc, and if the opportunity to get to Saigon came up, as usual I would skip the King Bar in favor of some jumps with the Vietnamese.

****

It was not a great distance down the highway from Thu Duc to Saigon but the highway was not secure. The trip was best made by at least two heavily armed soldiers and a full tank of gas.

I enjoyed jumping with the Vietnamese. These jumps were what we called "Hollywood," which meant no equipment was required other than your helmet, personal weapon and, of course, a parachute The best part was that they were straight up and straight down without a field exercise or operation after the jump.

I had already met the strict requirements for Master Wings regarding types of jumps, such as night jumps, mass tactical jumps or combat equipment jumps as well as the requirement to be a qualified Jump Master. I just needed some more time on jump status and a handful more Hollywood jumps.

Like the weapons in the RVN arms rooms, the planes the Vietnamese jumped from were also WW II vintage; none more so than the C-46 and C-47. The more modern planes they jumped from were mostly already obsolete as far as we were concerned and these would be the C-119 and C-123. The old C-46 and C-47 were different in that they did not have an upswept tail like more modern airplanes. This required the jumper to have a three second extension added to his static line. Instead of the usual counting of four seconds before deployment of the chute, the jumper had to count seven seconds and the difference was both noticeable and quite scary.

The most fun jump I enjoyed with the Vietnamese was out of a C-47 with a load of leather helmeted nurses. The chatter on board before the jump sounded like the sound track from a Daffy Duck cartoon. The Vietnamese were way ahead of us in allowing female soldiers to jump out of planes.

Decades later when I saw the Mel Gibson film, "We Were Soldiers," I was reminded of another eerie sight I had seen in Vietnam. In the movie, Joe Galloway (played by Berry Pepper) was inbound to LZ X-ray on a chopper flown by Medal of Honor winner Bruce Crandel (played by Greg Kinnear). As they neared the LZ, Joe notices a string of twinkling lights moving along a terrain feature down below. When he asks about it, Crandel tells Galloway that the VC and NVA use candles to light their way while moving at night. One of our operations took us into the A Shau Valley towards the end of 1965. Camped for the night on a ridgeline, I looked across the valley and I also saw a line of twinkling lights moving along the parallel ridgeline. They were no threat to us since we were a deep valley away, possibly a mile, apart, but SFC Milender and I decided they needed some artillery fire to help them on their way. I called our new Red Hat 5 (Tex had completed his tour of duty and had returned to the States) and advised him what 5B and I were watching and requested a fire mission on the lights. Wherever they were, Red Hat 5 and the RVN battalion commander could not see what we were seeing and suggested perhaps it might be the stars in the nighttime sky. I assured him these twinkling stars were moving and again asked for artillery.

In the meantime, the RVN troopers with whom we were camped gave no indication that they saw anything. I gave Red Hat 5 the grid coordinates and minutes later a couple of 155 howitzer rounds from our supporting artillery several kilometers away roared overhead like freight trains and impacted in the vicinity of the lights. I called Red Hat 5 and advised the rounds were on target and the lights went out. I asked if more was on the way and was told that the artillery battery did not want to expend more ammo on a dubious target. Several minutes later the twinkling lights reappeared again moving towards wherever they were going. I began to wonder if these two ridgelines, theirs and ours, didn't meet up somewhere up ahead. The fact that nobody except SFC Milender and I were excited about what we saw caused me to wonder if it really had been enemy troops on the move. Just as I felt vindicated when the movie "Tora, Tora, Tora" showed the big white cross standing on the Kolekole Pass, I again felt vindicated when "We Were Soldiers" showed enemy moving at night with candles.

The next day, in the daylight, a look at my map showed that the two ridgelines remained separated at least until the map ran out. This operation eventually ended with no significant contact for us but as the book *We Were Soldiers Once, And Young* by Lieutenant General (LTG) Hal Moore and Joe Galloway, and the movie based on their book showed, there was significant contact in another Vietnamese valley, the Ia Drang, in November of 1965, for the 7th Cavalry Regiment of the U. S. 1st Cavalry Division and thousands of NVA regulars.

Everyone on jump status, wherever U.S. paratroopers are, has to make at least one jump every three months in order to stay on jump status. Failure to do so will terminate both a trooper's status as a paratrooper as well as the extra proficiency pay he gets specifically for jumping out of airplanes. Several of Team 162 advisors, who were not jumping as frequently as I, had planned a proficiency jump on December 28th to maintain their jump status. I decided to do that jump also. That would keep my own jump status alive until the 28th of March and give me April, May and June to accumulate the required total of three years on jump status. I only needed about a dozen more Hollywood jumps to get the required number of jumps, but in a worst case scenario, I would spend my five day R & R in Saigon and make a few jumps daily to get my numbers.

The year 1965 was when U.S. Army units began arriving in Vietnam on a regular basis. The 173rd Airborne Brigade had been in-country for a while. Elements of the 101st Airborne arrived as well as the 1st Cavalry Division, the 1st Infantry Division, the 25th Infantry Division, the Americal Divisions and others. Some company grade officers and NCOs who had been in-country as advisors were being swapped with officers and NCOs newly arrived with the U.S. troop units. This was done so that everyone who arrived together as members of a unit would not all DEROS (Date of Estimated Return from Overseas) together at the end of a year. Of course, replacements for Killed in Action (KIA) and Wounded in Action (WIA) would be coming through the system at an accelerated rate corresponding to the dramatic uptick in combat action contributing to increases in KIAs and WIAs. It was a great relief that no one assigned as an advisor to the RVN Airborne had been tapped to change places with a soldier of the same rank from newly arrived U.S. units. The U. S. Marines already had a large presence in Vietnam in the northern part of the country closer to the Demilitarized zone (DMZ). Their battles for control of the ancient Imperial City of Hue and the defense of their base at Khe Sanh were among the bloodiest fights of the war.

When not in the field or unable to get to Saigon, SFC Milender and I kept each other company. We were on our third captain and feeling like we were pretty much Vietnam experts. We talked about cars, family, sports and music. We never called each other by first names but he was one of the best friends I ever had. He was a hard core country music fan. He explained that country music reflected reality and he named his favorite singers and sang a few bars from a few songs. He had a pretty good voice. Much later when I had a wife, she and I became fans of country music to the extent we visited Nashville several times and even sat in the audience of The Grand Old Opry once.

After this lull in the action, Airborne Brigade advisors were briefed on our part in a large joint operation on the Bong Son

Plain in Binh Dinh Province in the II CTZ. Binh Dinh Province had a very long coastline along the South China Sea and I heard from veterans who went back to Vietnam many years after the war that some nice modern hotels had been built along this coastline for the enjoyment of the many foreign tourists who would visit the future Peoples Republic. Those of us heading into Binh Dinh Province in January 1966 would not be relaxing on the beach. We were about to participate in the largest search-and-destroy operation yet mounted in the war and it would involve U.S. units, primarily from the 1st Cavalry Division (Airmobile), and a number of RVN units including the Airborne Brigade, as well as units of the Republic of Korea (ROK).

The name of the operation originally was "Masher" but apparently President Johnson was so upset that an operation meant to bring peace and stability to the region (which it really wasn't) had such a violent sounding name. He and others felt that it required a more peaceful appelation so they added "White Wing" to the title and the operation was now called "Masher/White Wing."

The type of operation was a search-and-destroy; the tactical maneuver was a hammer and anvil. The 1st Cavalry Division would be the hammer driving the enemy towards the anvil, which would be the RVN and ROK troops. On January 28, 1966, the first official day of the operation, the 5th Battalion of the RVN Airborne Brigade was moving along the plain to our positions as the anvil. We were moving on flat land with a sprinkling of small villages spread along our front. As we approached the first village, machine guns and small arms along with the thump of mortars opened up on us. We returned fire and again used rice paddy dikes for cover. We took several casualties in the opening burst of fire. Red Hat 5 advised by radio that he had called for U.S. artillery support. A short time later he again called saying, "Our fire support request is denied. 1st Cavalry choppers are using the same airspace taking their troops to their landing zones. Use fire and maneuver to neutralize the enemy, over."

I gave the standard military reply, "Roger that!"

After an exchange of fire with Charlie, the RVN paratroopers with a determination I had not before seen fixed bayonets and performed a frontal assault on the village. As we began to enter the village, the enemy, as was his practice, ran out the back door. The firing petered out as our opponents, no doubt, headed for prepared positions in the next village. We left the wounded and dead in the company of our walking wounded and prepared to move on to the next village well aware of what was waiting for us. Unfortunately, no medevac could come in for our wounded for the same reason we could not get artillery fire. Approaching the next village, we again met a determined enemy firing small arms, rockets and mortars in our direction. As they opened up, we returned fire. Artillery support was still not available and another frontal assault was required to dislodge the enemy. We now knew for sure we would be fighting our way over, around or through every village or terrain feature between us and where we were supposed to be. Again, the walking wounded were left in charge of the dead and dying and we moved on to the next village. As we got closer, no one was shooting at us. We entered the village and noticed prepared defensive positions but nobody was manning them. There was no sign of life of any kind including civilians, dogs, cats or water buffalo. We took a break, drank water and reloaded magazines for the next fight. I gave Red Hat 5 a situation report (SITREP) on the condition of the company I was with and I heard John Milender do the same. The captain advised that he would let us know when artillery or air support would become available. Until then he said, "We're moving out!"

The preferred thought as we began to leave the safety of the uncontested village, was that the enemy bypassed this village and kept going. The less preferred thought was they bypassed this village and set up big time in the next one.

I was traveling with the 51st Company. It was commanded by a competent company commander but he was the one who appeared to least care for the American advisors. Still, he was my counterpart for the day and my place was with him. We managed to communicate with his broken English, my broken Vietnamese and hand signals when necessary. John Milender was traveling with the 52nd Company on our left flank. One reason we were able to take the first two villages was because we moved with companies abreast and were able to execute flanking maneuvers on the enemy as well as the frontal assault. Rested and reloaded we began to exit the village.

The Vietnamese Airborne had learned from the French that, just like the U.S. Airborne, leaders led from the front. A point man stepped out first followed by the 51st Company Commander, his radio operator, then me and my radio operator. As soon as we stepped into the open field we heard the thump of mortars followed by blazing automatic weapons. The distance to the next apparently hostile village was approximately 100 meters so the mortar rounds began to land quickly and they were sighted-in perfectly to impact where we would be as we left the village. I saw the point man and company commander go down followed by his radio operator, my radio operator and then me. The explosion shut down my ears and I could only hear a loud ringing and nothing else. Brave troops behind us risked their lives to drag us back behind the cover we had just left. I felt sticky blood but felt no pain. The only way I could tell where I was hit was by where the Vietnamese medics were applying bandages. We were semi-safe behind a mud hut just inside the village. My head started to clear and I knew that I had been hit in the left shoulder, left arm and pretty badly in the left thigh. Additionally, I saw missing fingernails on my left hand and felt the medics applying bandages around my neck.

After I was bandaged up, SFC Milender appeared and kneeling over me said, "*Trung Uy*, the Cav choppers are out of the way and medevac is coming." He no sooner said these words than his eyes got big and round, his mouth formed a perfect "O" and his left arm, still holding his rifle, shot straight up in the air and under his armpit I saw the exit wound of the round that killed him. I recall a medevac helicopter landing and a gunship or two flying cover as the Vietnamese began carrying me, my counterpart and the other wounded to the chopper. Additional gunships had engaged the enemy. I yelled back to my friend, "*Trung Shi*," and the reply of the Vietnamese carrying me was, "*Chet roi*" which translates, "Dead already."

****

Sergeant First Class John Emerson Milender from Counce, Tennessee, is remembered on Panel 4E Line 103 of the Vietnam Wall. Back in the U.S., after getting out of the hospital and a couple of months into my new light duty assignment, I received a letter from John's parents asking me how he died. The Army, no doubt, helped them find me. I decided not to answer that letter because I felt I was responsible for his death. If he hadn't searched me out on the battlefield to tell me medevac was inbound, he might still be alive. Jump ahead to summer of 2009, I was so consumed with guilt about not answering John's parents' letter, not to mention the guilt for my role in his death, I called the local Veterans Administration office and made an appointment to talk with a counselor. It really pained me to think that every day for who knows how long, John's parents crept up on their mailbox hoping to find my reply to their letter. After I poured my sad story out to the counselor, he told me, "It's not too late to write the family."

After I got home I thought hard about what the counselor, Doctor Steven Nettles, had said. I went on the Virtual Wall where I located John and saw that a nephew and grandson had left tributes to him. Their email addresses were both shown with their tribute and I sent an email to each of them. I told them who I was and that John was with me when he was killed and why I never answered the letter from John's parents. Shortly thereafter, I was swamped with emails from all manner of relatives of my friend John. Of course, his parents had died long ago, but no one was mad at me. I explained to anyone who asked what John and I were doing when he was killed and that he died giving me aid and comfort. I heard from John's sister, daughters, nephews and cousins for weeks thereafter. Contact has since tapered off but I still hear from John's people, particularly on Veterans Day.

Six

Evacuation, Repair and Return to Duty

I GUESS I WAS IN SHOCK FROM BEING WOUNDED and seeing my friend killed. The medevac ride seemed short and neither my counterpart nor either of the two radio operators moved while lying on the floor. I couldn't tell if they were dead or alive and, apparently, I was the lone medic's priority at the moment. The point man, the first to step out from behind cover, was killed on the spot and was not on this flight. While the medic was sticking some sort of drip into my arm, I checked to see if I still had my pistol. I had brought this Colt 1911 Commander in 9mm into Vietnam with me since, at that time, it was not prohibited. Shortly after arriving in-country, bringing a privately owned firearm into Vietnam became prohibited, causing me to wonder how much trouble was I going to have getting it out of country.

When the chopper landed, just like the TV show "M*A*S*H," a crew in scrubs was waiting at the helipad and I was rushed onto a gurney and pushed into the field hospital. None of the Vietnamese got off with me and I've always wondered where they were taken. As I was wheeled along, I felt my uniform being cut off me and also the straps of my shoulder holster being cut and my pistol being removed. That alleviated my concern about getting the gun back home because I never saw it again. Next thing I know, I'm on a table and a nurse is telling me to count backwards from ninety-nine. I think I got to ninety-seven and it was lights out. I woke up in a recovery room. A nurse told me the surgery went well and I was at the 85th Evacuation Hospital in Qui Nhon, but I wouldn't be staying long.

The increased intensity of combat in II CTZ at this time was sending many more WIA troops to the evacuation hospitals than they can handle. A decision had been made that those who were safe to move would be flown to Clark Air Force Base in the Philippines to make room. That flight took place overnight and we were all moved into WW II type barracks. The next morning I awoke and saw I was on a cot in the middle of a long row of wounded. These cots went from wall to wall on both sides of the building. No one was talking and I didn't hear any moaning or screaming, but that was about to start.

A door to my left at the end of this long hospital bay opened and a group wearing white coats walked in and moved towards the first cot on the far side of the room. The first couple of white coats had scissors and stethoscopes. One of them had a clipboard, and lastly came a white coat pushing a cart with a large plastic barrel. The barrel guy positioned himself at the foot of the first cot and then the screaming began. The scissors guys began cutting bandages off wounds in order to examine the extent of damage. The blood soaked bandages went into the plastic barrel. This, I supposed, was triage to determine whose wounds were minor enough that they could return to their units after treatment and a brief period of rest; whose wounds were serious enough that they needed more surgery before going back to the war, which would be take place in Japan; and whose wounds were serious enough that they would be evacuated to a military hospital nearest their homes back in the States. The war would be over for that last category of soldier. The guy with the clipboard was in charge of writing down the destination of each soldier examined.

As the blood soaked bandages (which were applied as recently as the day before) were cut off wounds (inflicted as recently as yesterday or the day before), soldiers screamed, cursed and cried. The dried blood and gauze bandages could not be separated without causing severe pain and new bleeding. I lifted the sheet covering me and looked at the wound in my left thigh. The bandage was wrapped from just below my crotch to just above my kneecap. The dark red stain on the bandage ran almost the length of the dressing and was about three inches wide in the center. I thought, *Not even counting the bandages around my neck, my left shoulder and upper arm, these bastards in white coats are going to hurt me.* Removing the bandages from the fingers that lost nails wasn't going to be any fun either. I watched them move along the row of soldiers across from me leaving a trail of screaming, crying and very unhappy warriors behind them. All the while, the white coat with the clipboard penned in their next destination.

By the time they got to the end of the line of men across from me, I was exhausted from their pain and petrified thinking about what they were going to do to me. The white coats crossed over to my side of the building and began moving their reign of terror in my direction. Then, an apparent miracle happened. I can only guess that the white coats themselves became exhausted from the pain they were inflicting. Except for some sniveling and whimpering, the loud screams tapered off. I listened carefully and it seemed the doctors were now making their determinations based on the extent of the bandaging and the size of the blood stain. As they formed around my cot, I was afraid they'd go back to their old ways. I had the sheet off my leg exposing the blood stained bandage. A doctor eyeballed this largest wound and then looked at the lesser wounds. He then looked at the clipboard guy and said one word, "CONUS." That is military talk for, the Continental United States. I was going home.

The next day, those of us going to Japan for additional treatment or to the States were taken by buses converted to ambulances to the airfield. This was the first time since I was a baby that I was lifted and carried everywhere I needed to go. The C-130 transports were also rigged for medical transport like the one that brought me. Two planes were being filled and I hoped I was on the one headed for CONUS.

The stretchers were securely put in place on the aircraft. I assumed there were seats somewhere for the medical staff and air crew but from where I was, everyone I could see was lying on a stretcher. That is, with the exception of the poor fellow beside me on the other side of an aisle the medics used to move from patient to patient. He was suspended in something called a Stryker frame. Except for an occasional moan, it didn't appear that he could do anything else. Every so often, a nurse would turn this frame over, sort of like a rotisserie. I believe this unfortunate man had a broken back or a serious spinal injury. He didn't look good.

Frequently a nurse would come down the aisle and massage our butts. This was a very welcomed act not just because she was the first round eyed woman to lay a hand on any of us in months, but also because we laid on our backsides for so long that our butts really needed massaging. I was a little embarrassed during the butt rub because I was still wearing the same undershorts I had put on prior to deploying on Operation Masher/White Wing. I thought somewhere along the line I should have been given hospital PJs or something. But, on reflection, no one else had hospital PJs. I was sure this would be rectified when I got to a real hospital.

En route to CONUS, the plane touched down at Hickam Air Force Base on Oahu, Hawaii, to refuel. While we were stopped, an Army colonel got on the plane and started going from man to man. When he got to me he asked, "Did you get the Purple Heart?"

I replied, "Yes, sir." Only afterwards I noticed, if a soldier answered, "No, sir," the colonel pinned the medal on his bed sheet and a lieutenant with a clipboard jotted down some notes. I realized then that I should have answered "No, sir," because I had earned but not yet received the medal. I interpreted his question as, "Were you wounded in combat or hit by a jeep?" Well, I was too embarrassed to call him back. The medal and ribbon can be bought in any military clothing sales department of any Post Exchange back home. The important thing is having official orders awarding the medal. I was confident that the Airborne Advisory Detachment would take care of this important detail for me.

After a while, the plane took off again, destination, according to the nurse, McChord Air Force Base near Seattle, Washington. On arrival at McChord, we were loaded on bus-ambulances and taken to Madigan Army Hospital at nearby Fort Lewis, some of us only for the night, but for others living in the Great Northwest, it would be their home until their medical problems were resolved. The rest of us would continue moving eastward. For the night, I was taken to a real hospital room that I would share with an older guy already occupying a bed. I was helped into some blue hospital PJs and then into the other bed in the room. When the help left the room, I said, "Hi" to my roommate and he returned the greeting.

Then, a cheerful lady, probably in her early forties, came into the room with a basket of fruit. "I am so glad you are back from Vietnam, welcome home. How were you wounded?" she asked as she handed me a bright red apple.

"We were leaving a Vietnamese village," I said, "and we were fired upon by mortars and machine guns. I was hit in the neck, shoulder arm and leg, but my team NCO and friend was killed." I think that was much more information than she wanted but she said, "Oh, you poor man," as she turned her attention to my roommate. "Here's an apple for you, soldier," she said to him. "And how were you wounded?"

"I wasn't wounded, ma'am. I'm assigned here at Fort Lewis and I broke my foot in the motor pool," he said.

"Well," said the woman, "I'll need that apple back for a wounded soldier." As my roommate handed the apple back to her, I said, "I don't really like apples," and tossed my apple into her basket. She left the room.

When I was being wheeled into the room, I spotted a pay phone not too far down the hallway. It occurred to me that I had to let my parents know what was up with me before they got the telegram. Leaning against the wall near my roommate's bed were a pair of crutches. I asked him, "Do you mind if I borrow your crutches to get to the pay phone down the hall?"

"Man," he asked me, "do you think you can make it?"

"I think I can," I replied. "If you hear a loud clatter coming from the hallway you'll know I was wrong."

"Go ahead," he said, "but be careful."

I eased my legs over the side of the bed and my feet touched the floor. Using the headboard of my bed for support, I gingerly put weight on my right leg and reached for the crutches, managing to get one of them under each shoulder. So far, so good. Then I crutched my way out of the room and across the hall to the far wall, the side of the hall where the phone booth was located. I focused on the phone booth and, hugging the wall with my shoulder, began moving towards it. Then I started sweating profusely as I noticed, no matter how much I inched my way towards the phone booth, it wasn't getting any closer. I began getting dizzy and then I made the clatter that would signal to my roommate that I did not make it. The next thing I know, two hefty orderlies were helping me up and a third arrived with a wheelchair. As they put me in the chair, I looked back at the phone booth and I saw I had made some progress but I'll never forget how far away the damn thing looked just before I fell down. The orderlies and a disapproving nurse not only tucked me back into bed, they erected adult crib rails around me so I wouldn't try to get to the phone again. I told the nurse why I needed to make a phone call but she replied, "Your people will be notified by telegram. In fact, they probably have already. Just relax, you'll be heading home tomorrow."

I don't know when the telegram arrived at my parents' home in Arlington, but they did get one. My mother told me later, "I was on my way to work when this Yellow Cab pulled up to the curb. The driver got out and I thought he was going to ask me for some directions but then he waved this Western Union envelope at me and said it was a telegram for me. I told him I was running late for work and I'd read it later, but he said, 'Ma'am, I think you should read it now.'" Just like in the movie, "We Were Soldiers," the bad news was delivered by Yellow Cab.

****

Before long I was airborne again, only this time with fewer patients on board. The soldier in the Stryker frame was gone. The next stop was the Military Medical Center at Lackland Air Force Base in San Antonio, Texas. It was another over-nighter for those of us continuing east but it was the dropping off spot for soldiers who lived in this part of the country. Again, back in a barracks type building with a row of beds side by side, but this time with many fewer patients than started on this journey. Again, we were confined to our beds with no chance to make a phone call. I'm sure we were fed all along on this long trip, but I cannot recall eating a single thing either on the plane or any of the overnight stops. Lights were turned off and that was our signal to go to sleep. With the exception of those few words I spoke with my roommate in the hospital at Fort Lewis, there had been no conversation of any kind amongst us patients. It wasn't prohibited; I just guess nobody felt like talking. Everyone was probably still contemplating whatever trauma put them there in the first place.

All of a sudden, a voice from the bed on my right asked, "How did you get wounded?" I started to reply with the words most often used to answer that question, "We were...," but I was rudely interrupted by a loud voice from the darkness saying, "Shut the fuck up!" I was livid. I am an officer and the odds are that was an enlisted troop who yelled that. I started to think of something to yell back but a wiser voice somewhere in my head told me, "Forget about it." That's what I did. I could have started an argument I could never win.

The next morning, we were off again. I felt sheepish about starting to tell a war story last night in a room full of wounded warriors. I wondered if the asshole who yelled at me was on the plane or if he stayed in Texas. But for future reference dear reader, almost every war story you will ever hear starts out with "We were...." Choose one of the following:

a. leaving the village...
b. entering the building ...
c. kicking their asses...
g. getting our asses kicked...

****

Finally, we were airborne again with a much smaller passenger load. For this entire trip I assumed I was headed for the Walter Reed Army Medical Center in Washington, D.C., but I was pleasantly surprised to learn I was actually going to De Witt Army Hospital at Fort Belvoir, Virginia, located in Fairfax County, which is next to Arlington County. *It will be much easier for my family and friends to visit me at Belvoir rather than Walter Reed* I thought. I learned about going to De Witt instead of Walter Reed while the plane was stopped and unloading at Andrews Air Force Base in Maryland, just across the Potomac River from Virginia. Everyone was unloaded before me and placed into a bus-type ambulance. As I was being carried down the steps, I was wondering why the doors on this ambulance were closing and it began moving. Then, as the bus was pulling away, I saw a smaller military ambulance sitting on the tarmac. It was olive drab (OD) in color, a late model Pontiac station wagon type vehicle. If it had been painted black instead of OD, it surely would have been called a hearse. Then I saw painted on the driver's side door, DE WITT ARMY HOSPITAL, FORT BELVOIR, VIRGINIA. Two very polite men dressed in hospital blues opened the back door of the Pontiac and slid me into the passenger or patient compartment. I don't know how they expected me to be packaged when I arrived, but I was still lying on a standard Army field stretcher. Every previous medical conveyance I rode in was modified to hold and secure these stretchers. The Pontiac was not. They apologized for the ride I was about to take as the metal feet of the stretcher slid to the left or right depending on the turns the vehicle made. Along the highway straightaways, I lifted my head to peer out the window. It was February and there was still plenty of snow on the ground but not on the highway. I was happy to be home. *Maybe at De Witt I can call my parents.*

De Witt was not a big hospital because, as far as Army posts go, Fort Belvoir is not a big installation. Back in 1966, military hospitals had officer-only wards and separate wards for NCOs and enlisted. The officers' ward was numbered 5A, my former radio call sign. The ward was almost full but by no means crowded. I felt quite lucky to be placed in a bed at the end of the ward right beside a big window. Perhaps the word was out that a lieutenant wounded in Vietnam was coming into the ward because a lot of eyes were on me as I was wheeled to my bed. What I noticed about the other occupants of Ward 5A was that there was no way any of them recently arrived from Vietnam. They looked more like WW II or Korea Vets, and it was doubtful that any of them could be a lieutenant or even a captain. Later, a nurse told me, "The average rank of the other occupants of Ward 5A was lieutenant colonel and the most serious ailment was hemorrhoids."

I was wheeled into an examination room the next day and a surgeon explained what had been done to me at the 85th Evacuation Hospital and what was going to be done to me here. "Hello, Lieutenant Cavoletta, is that a proper pronunciation of your name?"

"No, sir, it's pronounced Colavita."

"Good," he continued. "The evacuation hospital removed a sizeable piece of metal from your neck. The treatment notes accompanying you said you were extremely lucky because the fragment didn't penetrate very deeply into your neck and hit nothing vital. As you get older and develop wrinkles, no one will even see that scar." He laughed, thinking he said something funny. "They also removed fragments from your left arm and you were lucky here too because the fragments sliced some tissue and muscle but didn't hit the bone. That wound is healing nicely from the inside out and we don't see any need to reopen it, although you will have an interesting scar there. The wound on your shoulder was a clean slice with no metal to be removed. Your fingernails will grow back without problems. Now, however, your thigh still has fragments in there so we are going to operate and get as much of the metal out of there as we can. You may still carry some of it with you when you leave here but the particles will be tiny and I don't see it causing you any trouble in the future."

"Do you see anything about these wounds that can screw up my Army career?" I asked.

"I do not," he said. "After your thigh heals sufficiently, you will be released on medical leave and later, when we remove the sutures, we'll make a final assessment. But I believe you will make a complete recovery from your wounds. You will, however, carry a medical profile for six months to a year which will cause you to be placed in a light duty assignment after you are released from the Medical Holding status. Your surgery is scheduled for tomorrow at 0900 hours. Do you have any other questions?"

"No sir," I replied.

"A day or so after surgery we will issue you a pair of crutches and later a cane. During this period of recovery I urge you not to engage in any grabass." Again he laughed and this time I laughed with him.

During my time at De Witt, my parents and brothers came to visit as well as my friends and girlfriends, current and former. Another frequent visitor was the Catholic chaplain. I don't know if he enjoyed my company or if he wanted to save me, or maybe I was the only Catholic in the ward. If he snuck up on me, I put down my book and chatted with him. If I saw him coming first, I sometimes played like I was sleeping. I thought about telling him that brother Frank and I got pressed into service as altar boys while we were in Hawaii. This actually happened at Fort Ruger about a year before we returned to the mainland. Our mother volunteered us after the previous altar boys, also brothers, went back to the States with their parents. My father rarely went to church but my mother was Irish Catholic, born in Belfast, Ireland. She dragged us to the post chapel for Mass every Sunday. The post chaplain was also Irish and a good friend of my father's, but not because of church. Their friendship came about at the Cannon Club bar while my father was the club officer and Father O'Reilly was a frequent bar patron.

I know Father O'Reilly was a good chaplain and a good Catholic, but he shook up Frank and I during Mass one Sunday morning. Preparing to walk onto the altar this particular Sunday morning, Father took his place behind Frank and I as we walked out of the dressing room and onto the altar. Frank and I noticed that the priest was not wearing an ornate outer garment over his white robe but we figured he knew what he was doing. We kneeled in our spots as Father walked between us up to the front of the altar. As he picked up the chalice, I guess he saw a reflection of himself and realized he had forgotten something. He turned his head, and over his shoulder whispered to Frank, "Get my robe." Frank motioned for me to come with him so I got up, genuflected and with our hands in the praying position, we both walked back into the dressing room and went to the holy clothes closet. Neither of us new exactly what he wanted but Frank took a vestment off the hanger, I draped it over Frank's still praying hands and he walked to the doorway where Father could see him as he lifted the garment up. Father O'Reilly, in the meantime, had been going on with the Mass like nothing was wrong. Father glanced at the garment and shook his head, "No." As Frank stepped back, I stepped forward with another vestment and held it up hoping for an approving smile. Instead of the smile, Father whispered, "No, goddam it!" "Holy shit," I thought, almost out loud. I was shocked. A priest using the Lord's name in vain in church, at the altar, during Mass? Fortunately, the next thing Frank held up was acceptable. We went back onto the altar and Father slipped into it without missing a beat. On reflection, I decided not to tell the De Witt chaplain the altar boy story. The leg surgery was painless because I was unconscious. Afterwards, the wires from the sutures tended to get stuck in my pants but I quickly learned to get along with them. Around the end of February, I was released from the hospital on two weeks medical leave.

****

It was now time to deal with Infantry Branch about my next assignment. They were aware that I needed a light duty assignment for from six months to a year. I again asked if they had anything in or close to Arlington. Let me state here for the record, always asking for jobs close to friends and family is generally not a good idea and I vowed to try to break that habit. Infantry Branch did, however, have a job that qualified as light duty and the assignment officer told me, "It's only about an hour away."

The U.S. Army War College in Carlisle, Pennsylvania, had a vacant slot for a branch chief in the Administrative Branch of the college. I didn't want to push harder so I said that job was fine with me. That made the assignment officer happy. Of course, as branch assignment officers tend to do, he shaded the truth, because on a good day, Carlisle, Pennsylvania, is at least two hours away from Arlington. My reporting date was March 14, 1966.

Carlisle Barracks, home of the Army War College, is a small campus-like post. At that time, the borough of Carlisle, west of Harrisburg, was somewhat famous for hosting the Washington

Redskins' summer training camp at Dickinson College. In the summer, it was a common sight to see the giant Joe Jacoby or some of the Hogs walking down Main Street in shorts and flip flops. The residents of the post were primarily War College staff and faculty plus the student body which was made up of lieutenant colonels and colonels who were there because they are the chosen future leadership of the Army. Other entities on post included a small detachment of military police charged with keeping the teenage children of the students in line. Also living on post were doctors and dentists who worked at the small post medical facility. My administrative staff were mostly civilians and all longtime residents of Carlisle. I also had two soldiers assigned, a sergeant and specialist fourth class who worked in classified document control.

Equipment assigned to the document control section included a brief case with a single cuff and chain attachment, and a short barreled .38 Smith and Wesson revolver. Somewhere in the immediate vicinity, I assumed, must be at least six .38 rounds, but I never saw them. In fact, during my tenure, no one checked out the briefcase or the gun. This was not a career enhancing job for an Infantry lieutenant and I was counting on the Combat Infantryman's Badge, three Bronze Stars, two with the "V" device for valor, and a Purple Heart to keep me competitive. The job did allow me to leave for the D.C. area right after work Friday afternoon, returning late Sunday evening. I wasn't even on any duty rosters.

The commandant of the War College at that time was Major General Eugene A. Salet. His previous assignment was commanding general of Fort Gordon in Augusta, Georgia. I learned later that he was a product of ROTC and not a West Point graduate. It was pretty rare to find a non-USMA graduate in the Infantry wearing stars. When he left Fort Gordon, the general took with him Sergeant First Class James Dumas, his driver, and Major Charles (Chuck) Hammaker, his Public Information Officer (PIO). I met

Sergeant Dumas first. He seemed quite friendly with a good sense of humor. Apparently, he just wanted to meet and greet the new lieutenant just back from Vietnam. Next, I met Major Hammaker who also seemed like a good guy. Then, things started to go south for me. It seems some busybody overheard the wives of the two current aides-de-camp to the general complaining in the commissary about the demands the general and his family made on their husbands' time. This person made sure Mrs. Salet heard about the complaints and Mrs. Salet told the general.

The commandant, who was also the installation commanding general, was authorized two aides, a captain, who was his senior aide, and a first lieutenant, his junior aide. Additionally, there was a brigadier general who served as deputy commandant who had his own aide, a first lieutenant. The deputy commandant's aide was a bachelor.

General Salet decided, after hearing about the complaining wives, that he wanted two new aides and both had to be bachelors. Officer promotions Army-wide had been accelerated. A number of factors caused this, beginning with company grade casualties from Vietnam and resignations and retirements because of Vietnam. I had recently found out that I would be promoted to captain in July. Apparently, SFC Dumas and Major Hammaker also knew this and they began to encourage me to interview for the senior aide job. One reason the generals' aides were on the clock such long hours had to do with the War College curriculum.

Weekly, and sometimes more often, very important people in government, particularly from the Defense and State Departments, were guest lecturers at the college. Usually, the evening of a VIP's visit to the college, the commandant hosted a dinner for them at Quarters One. Rarely, the deputy commandant would host the dinner at Quarters Two, but when he didn't, he was always a guest for the dinner at Quarters One. General Salet believed the aides would benefit by being at these dinners, so all three aides were required to be present. The aides did not eat at the same table with the distinguished guests but they did mingle at cocktails before dinner and after dinner for cigars and more drinks. If I had that job, my weekends in the D.C. area would be over.

After encouraging me to apply for the aide's job, they moved on to *strongly* suggesting that I should seek that position. In addition to putting some pressure on me to interview for the job, they also talked up the many benefits that came with the job of senior aide to the boss. In a way, I was flattered that SFC Dumas and Major Hammaker had found me suitable to join their group. I decided I would interview for the job; after all, I might not get it.

I got the job. To General Salet's credit, he did not hold the wives' complaining against their husbands and sent them both off to career enhancing jobs elsewhere. I think one reason the general liked me was that I had been in combat. The Army's efforts in Vietnam were still primarily advisor jobs and not that many junior officers had yet seen combat there. General Salet had seen combat both in WW II and Korea. He wore the combat patch of the 3rd Infantry Division on his right shoulder. Although he didn't wear jump wings, he still was a member of the Airborne fraternity.

He wore the Glider Badge that signified Airborne soldiers who flew into combat on gliders. These were plywood, engine-less airplanes towed into battle behind a motorized aircraft. Many of the men who rode these gliders to meet the enemy were killed or seriously hurt when their glider flipped over on landing, or came in too hard and broke apart, or struck an immovable object on the ground.

The junior aide selected by the general was a very sharp first lieutenant named Jim Bryant. He was a West Point graduate and his father, a retired three star general, was a former commandant of the USMA. Jim and I shared the aide-de-camp workload and became good friends.

The first time I walked our general home after work, I declined his kind offer to come inside for a drink. I wanted, instead, to take my new Harley Davidson Sportster for a ride in the hills around Carlisle. The next day, Major Hammaker and SFC Dumas advised me that I had made a bad error in judgment by not having that drink with the general. They advised the next time, and every succeeding time, I was invited, I needed to have that drink. The first time I joined the general for a drink he asked what I would like and I said, "A bourbon and coke, please." The general said, "That's a waste of good bourbon." He poured some scotch over some cubes and said, "Tell me what you think of this."

Immediately light headed I replied, "I like this."

The next time I walked him home he mixed me a dry martini and asked, "How about that?"

I replied truthfully, "I liked the scotch much better."

He was pleased with that and I have been a scotch drinker ever since.

My comment about Jim Bryant and I sharing the load was especially true when it came to walking the general home after work because whichever one of us did, the rest of the evening was shot. We would be close to shitfaced as we walked the short distance from Quarters One to the Bachelor Officers Quarters (BOQ). A TV dinner and early bedtime usually followed. Jim Bryant also had a motorcycle but due to the fact we alternated walking the general home, we rarely rode together during the week.

****

There was another member of the general's team who had to let me know she had clout. This would be the commandant's secretary, Vickie Martin. She did not accompany the general from Fort Gordon but was a local Carlisle resident who worked her way up her career ladder to this position. She had been secretary to the previous commandant and would be secretary to the next commandant. I liked her very much and enjoyed sharing an office with her. But she too had to demonstrate how she could help me or hurt me. Shortly after I became the general's senior aide, he was scheduled to visit nearby Fort Detrick in Maryland and we planned to leave from the office the next morning. That morning I showed up for work in my complete Class A uniform—shirt, tie, blouse and flying saucer hat. Right after I arrived, in came Jim Bryant wearing what would be the normal duty uniform for a warm day at the office—open collar short sleeved shirt, khaki trousers and the overseas cap. Then the general walked in wearing the same uniform as Jim.

"Rocky," said the general, "you look like some kind of goddam ballroom banana in that uniform. Jim, you're coming to Detrick with me," and they left. As I was standing there wondering what a ballroom banana was, Vickie said to me, "Oh Rocky, I'm so sorry. I forgot to tell you what uniform the general was wearing." And this coming from someone who never forgot anything! *Okay*, I thought, *message received.*

The bigger problem that Jim and I had to navigate was that Vickie didn't like Hammaker or Dumas and they didn't like her.

As time went on, Jim and I moved pretty well between the parties. The advantages of being the commandant's aide did indeed outweigh pub crawling in Georgetown. A pretty nurse named Nita assigned to the post medical center had moved into the BOQ directly over my room. We hit it off well and began dating. She knew that taking care of the general and his family had to be my number one priority but we still found time for fun. She loved my motorcycle. But all good things come to an end.

Abruptly, without any prior notice, General Salet received orders transferring him back to D.C. He was to run some weapons systems evaluation group and his departure was imminent. The new incoming commandant was a general named McCaffrey, a West Point graduate and the father of a son, Barry, who would make four stars before retiring after which he would regularly appear as a military analyst on network television. Incoming General McCaffrey communicated with General Salet and asked if his two aides, Jim and I, could remain in place until he got settled in. General Salet told me, not in the presence of Jim Bryant, "I'll be damned if I'll leave anything in place for that ring knocker (slang for USMA graduate). Jim needs to go to Vietnam, and I think he knows that, but where do you want to go?" I thought for a second and answered, "I would like to be assigned to the Airborne School at Fort Benning."

General Salet replied, "That's an unusually stupid request. I'll get you to Fort Benning but it will be to attend the next available Infantry Officer Advance Course (IOAC)."

From that point, things moved quickly. I received orders placing me in IOAC Class number 2-68 beginning October 3, 1967. I had just enough time to say goodbye to Nita, pack my stuff, acquire a trailer to move my cycle, and hit the road. I never saw Nita again, but during my second tour in Vietnam, a friend of mine who spent a short time at the 85th Evacuation Hospital in Oui Nhon told me he met a pretty nurse while he was there, named Nita. The 85th Evac Hospital, you recall, was my departure point from my first tour in Vietnam.

****

In the big scheme of things, going to the advance course ahead of my peers was a good thing. This would look good on my record because I was a junior captain attending the IOAC well ahead of my year group. The entire Carlisle Barracks experience had lasted almost exactly eighteen months: three months as admin officer and fifteen months as aide to the commandant. As far as my light duty medical profile, I never heard another word about it and I assumed it simply expired.

The IOAC began on October 3, 1967 and would finish on July 9, 1968. The class consisted of over 200 officers, mostly captains and a few majors, and ended as mostly majors and a few captains. In a big change from the Infantry Basic Course, most of the IOAC students were married, so the burden was on a small number of bachelors to uphold the unmarried Airborne Ranger tradition of coming to class with sunglasses on to hide bloodshot eyes.

Similar to the Basic Course, this class was about an even split of West Pointers and ROTC guys, but there was a third element that was not present in the basic school. These were former enlisted soldiers who received their commissions from Officer Candidate School (OCS). These guys looked a bit older than the college grads and some, while wearing short or rolled up sleeves, displayed tattoos such as a skull with a dagger sticking in an eyehole with something like, "Death Before Dishonor" written below. One thing we all had in common was that we had all been to Vietnam and we were all going back after graduation.

At the very beginning of the IOAC was a difficult block of instruction we all had to pass in order to move on. It was a newly developed course entitled, "Nuclear Weapons Employment." This was all about planning for the use of tactical nuclear weapons on the battlefield. Using a slide rule, we were supposed to be able to determine the maximum and minimum radii of damage depending on the size nuclear weapon we were using. (Note: The only time I ever even said "slide rule," let alone used one, was in a little joke: One moron says to the other, "I'm constipated, what can I do about it?" The other moron answers, "Work it out with a slide rule.") Well, believe it or not, I passed that block of instruction and was eager to move on to more pedestrian subject matter. It was, however, the nuclear weapons class that gave me another nickname which really saw little usage outside of me and my roommate and a couple of our close friends.

At the beginning of school, I was checking out the BOQ where I could stay during the course. It was the standard cinderblock room sharing a bathroom with a similar cinderblock room on the other side. I opened the bathroom door and came face to face with a big guy who extended his meaty hand and said, "Hi, I'm Ed Yago." I shook his hand and said, "Hi, I'm Rocky Colavita."

Ed said, "*Paisano?*"

I replied, "Fifty-fifty. My father's folks came from Italy but my mom is Irish."

"Rocky," said my new best friend, "we can do better than the BOQ. We'll be here into the summer and you know there's no air conditioning in these buildings."

"Roger that, Ed. Any ideas where we can look?"

"I heard some guys talking about a new townhouse development just off post called Wedgefield Court. Let's take a look."

We did look and ended up renting a nice, furnished unit between two sets of our classmates. One of these sets had to wait a couple of days before moving in because some fellows involved in the shooting of John Wayne's movie "Green Berets" were in the process of moving out. The movie was shot entirely at Fort Benning. Several more classmates moved into Wedgefield Court, some married with kids and more bachelors and roommates of convenience.

Now to the nicknames both Ed and I received. We called each other "Pies," obviously the shortened version of *Paisano*. But the other guys needed a way to differentiate between the two of us. Going back to the maximum and minimum radii of damage by a nuclear weapon, Ed became Pies Max and I became Pies Min. Most of us had a good time during IOAC. The instructors had to maintain control of their classes but they knew we had all been to Vietnam and were going back so they maintained a pretty relaxed environment, certainly more so than the IOBC.

Came the Christmas holidays, we all left for home. I never mentioned to my family that I knew I was heading back to Vietnam and we just enjoyed each other's company. After the holidays we all returned to Benning to continue class.

As spring arrived, many of us had been thinking hard about which unit to request going back into the war. You didn't have to request a unit, you could leave that to chance and the Army would pick one for you. You could even waste a request form by asking for an assignment to Hawaii if you wanted. No one intended to leave it to chance and no one was dumb enough to ask for Hawaii.

We would graduate in July and 1968 was already shaping up as one of the bloodiest years of the war. Having an Airborne background, I really wanted to request duty with the 101st Airborne Division. But, most of us in the class were Airborne qualified and I heard a lot of buzz about the 101st. Having been so lucky in getting an Airborne job with MACV, I felt I probably couldn't get that lucky again. Other Airborne choices were the 3d Brigade of the 82d Airborne Division and the 173d Airborne Brigade, but these were separate brigades, each one-third the size of a division, meaning fewer opportunities to command a company.

Finally, I settled on the 1st Cavalry Division (Airmobile). The Airmobile concept was being tested at Fort Benning while I was a student in the basic, Airborne and Ranger courses. Then, in

1965, what had been the 11th Air Assault Division (Test) was designated the 1st Cavalry Division and off they went to Vietnam. When they went over, the 1st Brigade was Airborne. I decided to request the Cav and hope for an Airborne slot, but if I didn't get one, I'd still be in light Infantry. I was happy with my decision and even happier when I learned I was indeed going to the Cav.

Seven

The Log Man

THE TRIP TO VIETNAM THIS TIME BORE NO RESEMBLANCE to my flight across the pond on an Air Force C-130 in 1965. This time it was aboard a chartered Continental Airlines passenger jet complete with stewardesses, inflight movies and meals. We took off from Travis Air Force Base in the San Francisco Bay Area. The civilian flight crew was upbeat and extremely pleasant as they interacted with us. In fact, they were so accommodating and friendly, they were acting like we were all terminal patients in a cancer ward. That's not a complaint! Rather than the all-business demeanor on a regular flight to some desirable destination, the stewardesses, all quite pretty, put their elbows on top of seatbacks and engaged in conversation with us. We enjoyed two or maybe three in-flight movies en route to the war and the meals were quite good. As we exited the airplane at Bien Hoa, the crew clustered around the door saying cheery things like, "Good bye, good luck, we'll see you on your flight back home."

After years of experience dealing with massive arrivals and departures of troops, the replacement depots at Long Binh and Cam Ranh Bay had made processing both in and out of country quick and almost painless. After a night's sleep in row after row of bunk beds, we would begin efficiently moving from the replacement depot to our newly assigned units. Throughout the Vietnam War replacements came in and left as individuals. Even though we flew to Vietnam on a plane full of other military men and women, each one of us was to fill a slot somewhere in the vastness of Headquarters, U.S. Army, Vietnam (USARV) or MACV. We came in alone and went home alone, which had its advantages and disadvantages.

Unlike previous wars where soldiers deployed with a unit and came home together as a unit, less those who became casualties, those returning from Vietnam might well be getting off a plane alone and entering a civilian airport where they may have had to face calls of "baby killer," "murderer," etc, and maybe even get spit on. Troops coming home after WW II on troop ships had the chance, along with their unit buddies, to decompress and get the war out of their heads before getting home. Additionally, they were all treated as heroes.

The advantage of the rotation of individuals out of Vietnam was that you didn't have to wait until a troop ship was filled and then spend days and days at sea before arriving home. In Vietnam when your DEROS arrived you were quickly flown out of the war zone and found yourself back home in a few short days. The WW II generation has become known as the greatest generation and I don't quarrel with that, but in my humble opinion, the generation that blamed the Vietnam War on the soldiers who fought it had to be the dumbest generation.

I didn't notice a single significant flaw in the in and out processing of soldiers until it was time for me to leave a year later. As I climbed onto my upper bunk I said to the young soldier in the bunk next to me, "I bet you're glad to be leaving this shithole," and he replied, "I just got here."

The 1st Cavalry Division ran The First Team Academy (FTA) in An Khe in the II Corps Tactical Zone. The initials for this training academy, "FTA," were unfortunate because if you saw "FTA" written on latrine walls anywhere else in the world where the U. S. Army was present, they stood for, "Fuck The Army." Officers and enlisted attended the same instruction in the FTA and it was primarily how to quickly board and get off helicopters, most notably the UHI-D, affectionately known as the Huey. Unarmed Huey helicopters configured for carrying troops were also called "Slicks."

At An Khe we had the opportunity to have our newly issued jungle fatigues affixed with sewn on division patches, name tags, rank and in my case, the Combat Infantryman's Badge, Senior Jump wings, a Ranger tab and the MACV patch with an Airborne tab over it, which I had earned on my first tour.

It was a private Vietnamese concession selling the patches and sewing them on and it wasn't cheap. But buying this service turned out to be a not too smart thing to do, as those of us going to tactical units in the field learned later. The first time you turned in a uniform to be laundered in the rear may well have been the last time you saw it. When freshly laundered uniforms came back, and I didn't know if they were done by Army Quartermaster people or contract Vietnamese, the important thing was to get a shirt and pants that fit and not to worry about previously sewed on items. Almost everyone went through the war with some uniforms without name tags, rank or anything else stitched on. I wondered for a while if some young private was walking around with one of my uniform shirts. Then again, maybe it was the laundry service cutting off the stuff people paid to have sewn on and re-selling it over and over.

A major exception to all this no-rank, no-name tag thing appeared to be senior NCOs and officers at the rank of lieutenant colonel and above. They always seemed to have their rank and name tags sewn on their uniforms. Towards the end of FTA training we were going to find out our specific assignments, at least down to battalion level. I had already learned that I was going to be assigned to the 1st Brigade, the one that came to Vietnam on Airborne status. And then I found out that the brigade's Airborne status had been scrapped shortly after arriving. Officers on jump status collected an additional $110.00 a month and enlisted soldiers collected $55.00 a month in jump pay, so this represented a significant cost savings for Uncle Sam. Despite the cost savings, I believed this decision to un-Airborne the 1st Brigade was properly influenced by the undisputed realization that the quickest, safest and best method of bringing a large number of troops to the enemy, in a hurry, and depositing them all close to where they were supposed to be, was by helicopter, not parachute. There were just too many trees in the Vietnam jungle for paratroopers to land in.

As an Infantry captain, my burning desire was to command a front line rifle company. A headquarters company wouldn't cut it. In the case of the 1st Cavalry Division, I wanted a front line airmobile infantry company. I was lucky to be a member of a highly mobile light Infantry outfit and my wish to never become intimate with tanks and armored personnel carriers and their maintenance and spare parts problems had again been granted. No Infantry captain worth a damn would want anything but to command a rifle company. We all knew that company command lasted approximately six months or less after which incumbents had to vacate these positions to give another captain a chance to be a commander. There were exceptions, of course, but that had more to do with a shorter period of command, shortened, for example, by getting killed or seriously wounded or being relieved for incompetence.

I was certain I would get my company command time but I had no idea if it would be near the beginning of this tour or towards the end or maybe six months out of the middle. And I wouldn't find out until I was assigned to a battalion. I also learned in the First Team Academy that, in the Cav, mortar teams and reconnaissance troops, formerly assigned to each line company, had been detached from these companies and formed up at battalion level in new company-sized units designated Echo Companies. While an Echo Company for me would be far better than commanding a headquarters company, I didn't want one of them either.

When the assignments came through, I was to be assigned to the 2d Battalion of the Eighth Cavalry Regiment. This battalion was operating near the city of Quang Tri on a Landing Zone (LZ) named Sharon in I Corps. If you wondered where the names of many of these LZs came from, they were often the first names of the wives of the first battalion commander who built and subsequently occupied the LZ. Protocol dictated that when the first commander leaves the firebase, the next guy who takes this particular LZ over cannot change the name and, unless he builds another one, his wife wouldn't get a firebase named after her. This was mainly due to the fact that once a firebase was built, occupied and named it was added to all maps of the division Area of Operations (AO).

At this point, let me make clear that an LZ, a firebase and a fire support base are basically the same thing. A named LZ, e.g., Sharon, is also a firebase and, if it has artillery on it, it is also a fire support base. So the terms firebase, fire support base and LZ are pretty much interchangeable. Un-named LZs are any place where helicopters can land. They may be natural clearings in the jungle or manmade by blowing down trees sufficient for at least one chopper to land.

On my way to LZ Sharon, I was mentally building my case to take command of a rifle company (my experiences on the first tour, early attendance at the Infantry Officer Advance Course, three Bronze Stars, two with "V" for valor, etc.) On my arrival I was escorted into the Tactical Operations Center (TOC) and introduced to the battalion commander, Lieutenant Colonel (LTC) Jack Gibney, and the executive officer (XO), Major Richard Fish. The battalion radio call sign was Stone Mountain, so I was in the presence of Stone Mountain 6 and Stone Mountain 5. For those not totally familiar with the Army, in order to shorten conversations, once an officer is known to be a lieutenant colonel, it is permissible to call him "colonel." Colonel Gibney told me that the line companies, Alpha, Bravo, Charlie and Delta, had relatively newly assigned commanders. The same was true of the Headquarters Company (thank God!) and the Echo Company (Yippee!) so I was being assigned as the battalion S-4, also to be known as Stone Mountain 4.

I never had a chance to reel off my resume qualifying me for command, but with a captain running each line company, it wouldn't have made any difference. The S-4 is the principal staff officer responsible for supply and logistics. Being assigned to the S-4 position did, however, give me cause for concern because supply, especially in the field, is where many unauthorized trades of goods take place which can land people in the U. S. Disciplinary Barracks at Fort Leavenworth, Kansas. An example of such a trade would be a deuce-and-a-half truck for six cases of scotch. I planned on being both watchful and careful in this job.

Although fighting had been fierce around LZ Sharon in the first half of the year, contact with the enemy in I Corps had tapered way off in recent months probably due to the thrashing the VC took during their Tet Offensive in the first part of the year.

The exception to a lack of combat action was the frequent dropping of rockets and mortar rounds on the LZ in the nighttime. For this reason, everyone slept underground, way underground. Major Fish arranged it so that I could move underground with a lieutenant from Personnel who shared a cave with his NCO. Within a week to ten days, another lieutenant from Operations was leaving and I would be moving into his hole in the ground. I had no idea what kind of hole the previous S-4 lived in.

The Personnel officer's bunker was almost luxurious. It appeared to have been dug with heavy equipment and then a roof made of pierced steel planking covered with earth and sandbags was laid over the excavation. Quite frankly, there was enough room in that hole for the original two inhabitants, me and one or two more guys. But, when the Operations lieutenant moved out of his hole, I moved in. And this was an actual hole dug by hand and quite deep. I slept on a GI air mattress lying on two wooden pallets to keep me out of the mud and water in the bottom of the hole. And this is where I lived for the next almost three months while I performed the duties of the "log man."

For several days in the beginning of my assignment, I heard about a mysterious helicopter called the C & D Bird. Timely departure and arrivals at the locations of each of the line companies in the early morning hours each day was crucial and it was my responsibility to see this mysterious flight stayed on schedule. Long before I had the guts to ask what, exactly, the C & D Bird was, I imagined such names as "The Casualty and Death Bird," "The Capture and Destroy Bird," or maybe "The Chink and Dink Bird." Finally, I asked my all-knowing property book officer, CWO Warren Prillaman, "What exactly is the C & D Bird?" He told me with a straight face, "It's the Coffee and Doughnut Bird." Then I said to him, also with a straight face, "You are shitting me, right?"

"No," he replied. "It's a morale thing. Fighting has slowed down so the colonel sends mermite containers of coffee and fresh baked doughnuts to each line company each morning. The chopper gets the coffee and doughnuts from the brigade mess at 0500 hours and then flies to each company location before they move out for the day on their search-and-destroy operations."

I was thunderstruck. *The fucking war is going to be over before I get my chance to command a company!*

Nothing much in the way of killing was going on by either side in I Corps but I was too busy learning the S-4 job to worry much about it. The first thing I did after learning I was the S-4 was write to Fort Benning to get enrolled in the Infantry Officers' Logistics Correspondence Course. Not only was the war almost over, but if I did get a company it was going to be full of guys fat from stuffing their faces with fresh baked doughnuts!

Then, things got worse. LTC Gibney announced that the division G-4 had scheduled the battalion for a Command Maintenance Management Inspection (CMMI) in a few days. The CMMI is a chicken shit inspection of all things in the battalion that require routine maintenance and spare parts. Most of this stuff was in my area of responsibility. This kind of inspection had been put on hold for most of the war so far and now it was coming back, another sure sign that the war was almost finished. So, we started checking off the things we had to accomplish in order to pass this CMMI, and then everything changed again. LTC Gibney was moved up to division G-3 and we got a new Stone Mountain 6, LTC Frank Henry.

Then we were told that the 1st Cavalry Division was moving south, lock, stock and barrel, to War Zone C in the III CTZ around Saigon. We were to establish a temporary division headquarters in the Michelin Rubber Plantation at Quan Loi. I was familiar with the rubber plantation because the RVN Airborne had been involved in operations there during my first tour.

We were trading the mountains for the jungle. That was fine with me. I had worked before in both the mountains and jungle and I preferred the jungle. Colonel Henry called me into the TOC. "Rocky," he said, "you're probably going to be the last man out of here. You need to plan for the out-loading of the entire battalion, men and equipment, by C-130. Then you and whoever you pick, will have to load up everything in our ammo dumps and bring it to the brigade ammo resupply point where it will probably be reissued to whoever replaces us in I Corps." That was a big order but I was so relieved that we didn't have to stand that crappy CMMI that I was ready to go.

There were templates in my *Logistics Officer's Handbook*, recently arrived from Fort Benning, for out-loading men and equipment on C-130s, so I was able to accurately advise Colonel Henry how many C-130 trips it would take move the whole battalion south. The ammo was a different sort of problem. We had no forklifts available to us and they wouldn't have mattered anyway because our ammunition—small arms rounds, mortar rounds, 7.62 caliber machine gun rounds, hand grenades and Claymore mines—had been removed from pallets and disbursed in pits dug into the ground to protect the ammo from everything except a direct hit by a mortar or rocket. A Claymore mine is a directional anti-personnel mine filled with C4 explosive and over 700 steel ball bearings. It is command detonated by a soldier sending an electrical charge by wire to a blasting cap inserted into the mine. It propels those steel balls over 100 yards within a sixty degree arc, unless, of course, the balls come in contact with trees, rocks or enemy soldiers. (I was to learn much more about Claymores in my immediate future.)

I took six guys from the S-4 section, requisitioned a five-ton truck and flatbed trailer from brigade and the seven of us manually moved tons of explosives from the ammo pits to the trailer. We drove all this the few miles to the ammunition supply point at brigade where we were met by, guess what, forklifts. The troops manning the fork lifts advised that they could not help us because the ammo wasn't palletized and they spun around their machines and headed back where they came from. We were supposed to manually unload the trailer and carry this stuff somewhere? I don't think so. So, as if practicing to be a company commander, I made a command decision with only passing thought to how much trouble I might get in. "Troops," I yelled, "unhook the trailer, we're leaving it here." We then drove the truck, with the cab full of people and others standing on the running boards, to the departure airstrip near LZ Sharon and caught the last C-130 lift to III Corps.

On the flight to Quan Loi and even later into the evening, I had some concerns, but no regrets, about leaving that trailer loaded with ammo exposed to incoming fire. Then again, if brigade gave a shit, they would have had some real assistance standing by to help us out. Surely, if some officer or NCO drives by and sees it, the trailer will get unloaded and the stuff placed below ground level. I believe I indicated earlier that the logistics field offers some unique opportunities to end up in jail. But, I never heard a peep about that loaded trailer.

After we landed, it was up to me and my guys to hitch a ride to the 2/8 area, which wasn't too hard to do. For my part, now that the line companies were off the mountains and into the jungle, I wanted to see how fast stupid shit like a C & D bird disappeared, not to mention something as ridiculous as a CMMI. I was really getting antsy for one of these companies to open up, not that I wished anything bad on any of the current company commanders. I just had to be patient.

Eight

Angry Skipper

I FOUND 2/8 TEMPORARILY OCCUPYING AN LZ NAMED Joe which was situated on the grounds of the Michelin rubber plantation. Although it was a common practice for the building and first occupying commander to name his LZ after his wife, it wasn't mandatory. In fact, if a particular commander wanted to name his LZ after his Cocker Spaniel, I imagine there could well have been an LZ Rufus somewhere in Vietnam.

LZ Joe was small and eerie. Although division headquarters and several other battalions were also on the grounds of the rubber plantation, Joe seemed remote and cut off. It had been built and operated by whatever outfit worked in this AO before the 1st Cav came south.

As soon as I reported in to Colonel Henry, he said, "Rocky, you're going to the field." All I could think of was that a complaint had come down from brigade about me leaving the trailer full of explosives and munitions exposed. But instead of an ass chewing, Colonel Henry announced, "You're the new

Angry Skipper 6. Captain Buddy Garner has been on the majors'
promotion list and his number just came up. Majors don't
command rifle companies so now Delta Company is yours." I
was surprised and very happy.

(Angry Skipper is the coolest radio call sign of all the 2/8
companies and now it was mine. I was now a "6." After slinging
around 6s, 4s, 3s and so forth, there is probably no need to do so,
but just so all are clear: The "6" is the commander and that's true
at all levels: division, brigade, battalion, company and platoon.
In my time in the Army, the "5" was the second in command, the
deputy or assistant or executive officer. As the British say, the
"2IC." This may not be true today because now there are Civil
Affairs guys, Cyber guys, Systems guys and who knows what
else. The "4" is, as I was, the Log Man or Logistician. The "1" is
the Adjutant, or Personnel guy, the "3" is the Operations guy,
and the 2 is the Intelligence guy. The 3 is actually the 6's right
hand man and may be the same rank as the XO. Lastly, the letter
"S" before the 1, 2, 3 or 4 means they are on the staff of a
commander who is of lesser rank than a general officer. A "G"
before those numbers means that 1, 2, 3 or 4 are on the staff of a
commander who is a general officer.)

Captain-now-Major Buddy Garner was well liked by his troops
and I knew they were all probably sorry to see him leave. All of
them were concerned with who or what was replacing him. A
hasty change of command ceremony was scheduled for the next
day on the LZ.

A typical change of command ceremony has the company first
sergeant taking the unit colors, the "guidon," from the outgoing
commander and presenting it to the new guy. Then, the battalion
commander says some nice words about the outgoing
commander. Then, the outgoing guy says some nice words about
the troops. Then, the battalion commander introduces the new

guy to the troops, and then the new guy says a few words to the company. Buddy Garner's words praising his former soldiers were sincere and his eyes glistened slightly while he was speaking. Colonel Henry's introduction of me included words to the affect that I had served in Vietnam previously and, he erroneously said, that I had been an advisor to a Vietnamese Ranger battalion. He told the troops that I had extensive experience operating in the jungle environment, and this was true. He mentioned the jungle, no doubt, to try and put their minds at ease with regard to their new commander and their new beginning of jungle operations.

My words were brief. I said I was proud to take command of such an outstanding company of men and, I added, I truly knew they were outstanding as I had observed them for almost three months while I was Stone Mountain 4. I did not correct the error of a Ranger battalion vs. an Airborne battalion. There was no Pass-in-Review for a number of reasons, among them were no band and no room. My experience as an advisor with the RVN, I'm sure, didn't impress the troops. It really didn't matter what the battalion commander said about me what or I said because these men would make their own determination as to whether I was any good or not.

I had not met Major Garner prior to the change of command and I wouldn't see him again until over thirty years later when several of the men from Delta 2/8 met for a reunion at Fort Benning. But before Major Garner flew off LZ Joe to his next assignment, we did chat for several minutes while he gave me some pointers on Delta Company's strengths and weaknesses. He also gave me some opinions regarding the company officers and NCOs.

After the ceremony, I met with Colonel Henry and his operations officer, Major Rod Grannemann, for a briefing about the enemy activity in our new AO. Major Grannemann had been Angry Skipper 6 before Buddy Garner. The colonel also told me Delta would man the perimeter defense of the LZ for a little while to give me time to get to know my platoon leaders, first sergeant and platoon NCOs. I was glad I worked mostly in the jungle on my first tour because most of these soldiers I just took command of knew only the mountains. I was going to teach them to move through the jungle the way I wanted them to move. Learning to work the jungle would indeed be a new experience of major proportions.

The call sign Angry Skipper, in addition to being cool, also gave the men a way to address me which was casual but in no way disrespectful. They called me "Skipper." I also found out years later, during the many Angry Skipper reunions we would enjoy in the future, that behind my back some of the guys called me "Skippy."

At one or another of these reunions, some of the guys admitted to me that they either didn't like me or they were scared of me. One fellow confided in me saying, "You were a better tactician than Buddy Garner but he was a nicer guy." After that I thought, *Good! My plan worked perfectly.*

Delta Company platoons also had names and call signs: 1st Platoon was White Skull, 2nd Platoon was Wild Cat and 3rd Platoon was Rifle Range. The platoon leaders answered to call signs Skull 6, Cat 6 and Range 6. None of those platoon call signs met the criteria for a secure radio call sign, but what the hell.

I mentioned earlier that mortars and recon platoons were consolidated at battalion level in an Echo Company. I was absolutely fine with this not only because I didn't want guys with heavy mortar tubes, base plates and mortar rounds clanking through the bush and slowing us down, but also because shooting mortars in the triple canopy jungle can be very tricky. I figured that the reconnaissance section of the Echo Company could handle any particular recon concerns that the battalion commander or S-3 might have, but with my own one hundred and twenty or so infantrymen, we could do our own jungle reconnaissance. The platoon leaders who came with the company were Lieutenants Douglas Magruder, Michael Johnson and Greg Armstrong. I disliked Armstrong immediately. He seemed to always have a wise-ass smirk on his face and he had a smart mouth. I also had some suspicions about Johnson, who was former Air Force enlisted, but I assessed Magruder as a capable and competent officer and it was obvious that his men had confidence in him and affection for him. That comes only after being in combat together and covering each other's backs.

Change comes suddenly and before I had a chance to test drive my new company off LZ Joe, Colonel Henry advised all company commanders that we were moving out at first light the next day to occupy an LZ named Rita. It was not a new LZ but one built and occupied by the 1st Infantry Division, "The Big Red One." We would be moving in as they moved out.

This LZ was often hit at night by mortars and rockets as well as frequently probed by the enemy. It would take aggressive patrolling around the LZ to get that under control. Operations on and around Rita initially would involve one company defending the LZ perimeter and another company constantly sweeping the area outside the wire at approximately the range of the enemy's 81mm mortars. People inside the battalion TOC would have to know at all times the location of this company sweeping around Rita at a closer-in distance to ensure there were no accidents. That left two rifle companies to Charlie Alpha (Combat Assault by helicopter) and conduct more distant search-and-destroy operations.

When we arrived at Rita, Delta Company took the perimeter and the three other companies would all roam the area outside the wire while the LZ was being rebuilt. The harassing fire and aggressive probes by enemy troops, while the Big Red One occupied Rita, necessitated a complete rebuilding of the TOC and just about all the perimeter two man bunkers. During the day, my troops helped with the manual labor, in particular, filling sand bags. Most of the heavy work was done by division's 8th Engineer Battalion. The engineers had their heavy equipment, such as bulldozers and road graders, lifted in and out by Chinook helicopters or a Sikorsky Skycrane. Thanks to the engineers, the work went smoothly and was accomplished quickly.

While doing LZ defense, something happened that I didn't expect, but I probably should have. Guys started coming up to me as I moved around the LZ and began making a case for themselves to be reassigned to a rear area job. One said, "Skipper, I been in the field for six straight months now and I'm beginning to get real scared." "I just got here and I'm real scared," I answered. "Suck it up soldier and keep doing what you're doing. You'll be fine." In another attempt, a different soldier tried, "Skipper, your XO used to be my platoon leader and now that he's in the rear, he could really use my help."

My company executive officer, Lieutenant Karl Derums, was put in the XO position by Buddy Garner. He had been a decent platoon leader, soon to make first lieutenant, and I saw no reason to replace him. Lieutenant Derums came out to LZ Joe when I assumed command and I told him then what I expected of him. Among the things he would do on my behalf was write letters to families of my men killed or seriously wounded. Other than sending him award recommendations from the field, usually scribbled on scraps of paper or torn pieces of C-Ration boxes, for him to formalize and send to the battalion S-1 to review and forward on to brigade, I didn't need much interaction with him. As long as the troops were kept supplied, getting paid, being put in for awards recommended from the field, with no one missing their five day R & R, and most important of all, no one missing their DEROS, I didn't have much need to communicate with him. In fact, I didn't really know where "the rear" was although I suspected it was at Quan Loi.

Karl did tell me that he was adequately staffed to do his job and as his people departed he would let me know and I would choose replacements based on longevity and job performance in the field. I advised the troop who thought the XO needed him that he really didn't. Most of these requests for transfer to the rear were trial balloons and the requestor was, no doubt, aware that he didn't have a chance in hell of being put in a rear job. As one guy was asking me about a transfer everyone else was watching. I knew coming into this job that I had to be hardnosed. A long time ago I heard somebody's theory of leadership that went, "If you go in hard, you can always loosen up later. But if you go in loosey goosey, you will lose control and never be able to regain it." I knew, and hoped they knew, that I was not there to be their best friend.

I also knew that taking silly chances myself, such as I did too many times on my first Vietnam tour, was not happening on this tour. I was responsible for the lives of husbands, sons, fathers and brothers, etc., and it was my job to perform our mission while keeping as many of these soldiers alive as possible. I also heard someone say that, "The Army is loaning you a company of fighting soldiers and you have an obligation to return that company to the Army in as good or better shape than when you got it." That sounds good but it is absolute bullshit. We would be operating in a free fire zone. That meant all civilians have been relocated and there's no one operating in our AO but good guys and bad guys. The good news was, with no civilians and villages to deal with, a My Lai massacre wouldn't happen here. The bad news was, we could be lying in ambush and bite the nose off of an enemy unit three or more times our size and then we'd be in for the fight of our lives. My hope was to return the company to the Army in just about the same condition as I received it. I knew that doing this job, in this part of the country, facing the enemy we were facing, it would be impossible not to have people killed or wounded.

Getting back to efforts to get a job in the rear, I really had only one case that gave me pause. An impressive buck sergeant named Williams pleaded with me to get him out of the field because he had served several months already, not just as a grunt, but as a squad leader. He had a wife, a son and a college degree. He felt he had a bright future in civilian life if he just didn't get killed in Vietnam. I told him that I didn't need a sergeant to work in the rear at this time. I did not mention that a major factor mitigating against his transfer to the rear, even if I had a job opening, was the fact that Sergeant Williams was an excellent squad leader and his leadership probably had already saved the lives of soldiers under his supervision. I advised him that when the time came that I needed a good junior NCO in the rear, I would strongly consider his request. In fairly short order, requests for rear jobs fizzled out as guys saw that it wasn't happening and no one was going anywhere.

My first sergeant was a Puerto Rican master sergeant named Ramon Cruz. He was detail oriented and always immaculate in his jungle fatigues. He still had his rank and name tag sewed on his uniforms. He had a bit of an accent and he also frequently blinked his eyes more, I thought, than the average man. The troops must have thought so too because they nicknamed this senior NCO "Blinky." We had just met when First Sergeant Cruz told me he would be leaving the company immediately for his sixty days of reenlistment leave back home in San Juan, Puerto Rico. I figured sixty days of leave plus the hassle of getting out of Vietnam and back to Puerto Rico, and a similar hassle getting back to Vietnam from Puerto Rico, I would not be seeing Blinky for a long time. Internal travel was quite the problem because it was similar to hitchhiking, only by aircraft. The most senior platoon sergeant was a leathery senior sergeant first class named Bruce Adams. He was to be my acting first sergeant while Blinky was gone. People either liked or hated Bruce. Mostly, they hated him. He was from the old school where you corrected a soldier's behavior by beating him up. I figured he was going to be an obstacle to me and how I wanted to run the company.

I was aware that, before I took command, Delta was being extracted from the field following a search-and-destroy operation. An extraction is the reverse of a combat assault. Choppers come in and lift out the maximum number of troops the aircraft can carry. If only two or three choppers can fit in the LZ, only a small number of soldiers will get out at a time. The number of soldiers on the ground diminishes with each outgoing lift. When that number of soldiers got small enough, the enemy was known to attack. That happened on this extraction.

Helicopters that had left the LZ with troops and were in the air were instructed to turn around and take the men back to help the troops still on the ground. Troops who had been safely returned to the firebase were ordered to get ready to go back to the fight as soon as the empty choppers returned to the LZ. During this fight at the extraction site, my soon-to-be acting first sergeant, who was still on the ground, fought well, as was his habit, and killed a number of the attackers. As additional troops were ferried into the fight, the enemy broke contact and disappeared. Finally, under the cover of Cobra gunships, all the soldiers were lifted out and were returned to LZ Joe. Shortly after their safe return, Sergeant First Class Adams put himself in for the Medal of

Honor. He did get a Silver Star for this action but no one with him on the ground could support an award of the highest medal for valor. That told me a little something about my acting first sergeant. I truly expected to be bumping heads with Sergeant Adams but instead, to my surprise and relief, he and I got along just fine and over four months later when Blinky returned from reenlistment leave, I would be sorry to see Bruce Adams go.

****

Shortly after we took over LZ Rita, Colonel Henry told me he was sending me out to OJT with Charlie Company for a couple of days. I would travel with the company command post (CP) and observe. The company commanding officer (CO) was Captain Mike Gonzales. This OJT would be an eye opener for me in that the way Gonzales ran Charlie Company in no way resembled the way I intended to run Delta Company. For the two days I traveled with Gonzales, the company took aerial resupply both days. Every day, rations and ammo were delivered by helicopter as well as mail and iced down duffle bags of beer and soft drinks. Then all the guys, with the exception of some troops doing perimeter security, would lounge around reading their mail, chugging beer or soda and eating. So every day on their route of march, C Company had to find a suitable landing zone in order to receive their stuff. If they couldn't find one they had to blow one with det cord (detonation cord) and C4 explosive. There wasn't going to be any of that for Delta Company, where the enemy could track your direction of movement and daily progress by the ins and outs of a resupply helicopter.

The real surprise to me was the nightly ambush. I witnessed the most idiotic thing when I saw C Company troops placing a flare trip wire across the trail in the center of the kill zone. This meant that instead of letting the kill zone fill up with enemy soldiers before blasting away, this ambush would get only the first few guys who walked into it and set off the flare. Half of the kill zone would not be used for killing anyone. This was not my company and I kept my mouth shut but damn near everything I saw Charlie Company do was not the way I was going to do anything. Then my thoughts went back to the mountains and the C and D Bird. It seemed to me that these troops had been spoiled in the mountains by getting treats, whether it was coffee and doughnuts or cold beer. I felt Charlie Company was in for a hard time in the jungle.

When I returned to the LZ after my period of OJT, Colonel Henry advised me it was time for Delta to get out of the perimeter guard duty and begin search-and-destroy operations. He cautioned me that after we offloaded the helicopters that would carry us into the bush, he wanted me to call in SITREPS personally, not my RTO, because he wanted to get used to the sound of my voice on the radio. Before we were to Charlie Alpha into the bush, I got my platoon leaders, first sergeant and NCOs together and told them how it was going to be:

> We will go as far as possible, distance and time wise, every day without taking any resupply. If we step in shit and need resupply, we'll call for it but if we can walk three or four days or more without having a helicopter come in and give away our location, that's what we'll do. That means we will not be reading either love or Dear John letters every day. We will not be receiving iced down duffle bags of cold beer or soda, unless it's some kind of special occasion and we're in absolutely no danger of being caught with our pants down. We will hang around af-

ter resupply only long enough for guys to open a can of C rats, eat something quickly, then take over the perimeter while other guys get a bite to eat. I want the troops to leave our cans, wrappers and other residue in a visible pile in a clear spot on the LZ. Then we will saddle up and leave the resupply location. If we are moving to some predetermined point and have to hall ass to get there, that's what we'll do. But, if we aren't in a hurry, we might quietly sneak back near the resupply point and set an ambush around that pile of trash for anyone who might try to find some leftovers.

I have some good news for the men and some not so good news. The good news is that I know how soldiers really hate being sent out, away from the main body on listening posts (LP) or for an ambush. I am offering D Company an alternative. For starters, I don't plan to use LPs. As far as ambushes are concerned, I would like to use company-size ambushes. All of us together in the 'bush. No one has to go out, do the 'bush and then try to come back into the company perimeter. So, here's my ambush proposal.

First, we will endeavor to find a good recently used trail every night, if possible, where there is a decent likelihood we can kill someone. If evening is coming and we haven't found one by ourselves, I will call battalion and ask if someone can go up in the Charlie Charlie (the battalion commander's Command and Control helicopter) and identify one for us. Once we find a trail showing recent use, one platoon will be on the kill zone, the other two platoons will wrap around behind the ambush and link up. We will be in the circled wagon posture, so to speak, with 360 degrees of security. My CP will be in the middle of the formation. After we pop the 'bush we will be in a position to defend ourselves if attacked. I will call this formation a Delta 'Bush because we will be forming the letter "D." If we find a good trail intersection, two platoons will put ambushes on the two different trails where they intersect. The third platoon will wrap around behind the two ambushes making contact with the last man in each ambush. We can call this the triangle 'bush.

Claymores will be the primary killer in these ambushes, followed by grenades and, lastly, rifle and machinegun fire. After we spring a 'bush, I don't plan to have anyone step onto the trail at night to see what we got. The smartest and safest thing to do is wait for daylight to check the damage. There may be some painfully wounded enemy out there but this is war. Any movement or sounds coming from the kill zone should be answered by lobbing grenades towards the sound. Any weapons, maps and the like to be collected can be better collected during daylight. How does that sound?

They actually seemed to be quite happy and excited about what I was proposing.

Okay, here's the bad news. These ambush formations made up of well over one hundred guys will only work with absolute noise and light discipline. Absolutely, no talking, no smoking, no snoring and no farting. I expect platoon leaders and NCOs to strictly enforce noise and light discipline. Think of it this way, anyone who breaks noise and light discipline is someone who is trying to get us all killed. If we don't have absolute silence, we will have to go back to the Fort Benning ambush doctrine. You know, the way you have been doing 'bushes which you hate and which scares the shit out of you. Why is it that the Infantry School solution for ambushing is small ambushes out away from the main body? It's because nobody at Fort Benning believes that over a hundred guys can pull it off in a company sized 'bush. A group that size can't possibly be silent. I'm standing here saying, we can do it. Any questions?

I am not mentioning this to the battalion commander or the S-3 or anyone else, including the other company commanders, and I'm suggesting that none of you talk about it with anyone outside the company. If we do this right and our enemy body count and weapons seized count skyrockets, and we're not losing troops to the enemy, no one will really care how we're doing it. In fact, maybe it will eventually catch on, but for now it's our little secret.

I had one last bit of info to share with my company leaders:

Guys, I know most of you have only operated in the mountains where you pretty much have to move single file. That is not how we're going to move in the jungle. We'll travel with three platoons abreast. We should barely be able to see the platoon on the left or right unless we walk into a clearing. We'll be moving on a broader front and that's going to mean three guys will be walking point, but if we walk into an enemy base camp or bunker complex, we're in a better position to return a heavier volume of fire from the front and to circle the wagons, or break contact, or even to attack. It may be rough at first but we'll get used to it."

My choice of movement through the jungle, quite obviously, came from my experience with the RVN Airborne only we wouldn't be carrying pots and pans or live pigs and chickens. Later, I got good feedback from Lieutenant Magruder and some of the NCOs. For some reason, and I wasn't surprised, I didn't hear anything from Armstrong or Johnson.

The next day, around 0700, I would take my first ride into the bushes with D 2/8. That evening before my first Charlie Alpha with my troops, SFC Adams and I walked the perimeter checking in with the men ensuring they had decided who would sleep when and who would stay awake until relieved. It wasn't pitch black yet but it was dark. The third bunker we snuck up on we found a soldier who should be awake but who was napping. SFC Adams and I saw this at the same time but Adams looked at me with his index finger to his lips indicating I should leave this to him. I did.

Adams lifted the soldier's cased gas mask from where it was lying on the bunker and whacked him across the back of his head. The soldier fell forward but quickly turned with his hands in the air begging, "Please don't kill me." As soon as he saw it was the CO and first sergeant he looked relieved and embarrassed at the same time. SFC Adams gave him some career counseling and we continued our tour of the perimeter.

We had three listening posts out in the tall grass about fifty meters or so off the LZ in front of each platoons section of the perimeter. I know I promised not to use LPs in the field, but we were not in the field. We were still on the battalion LZ and it was the battalion commander's call. He wanted LPs out. For their own safety, the LPs had to be absolutely motionless and silent. They had radios to communicate in an emergency. In the absence of an emergency, they were to break squelch twice on this radio rapidly every half-hour. This told the soldier monitoring their radio that they were awake and all was well. As we approached the bunker where a soldier was monitoring the radio for Wild Cat's LP, he announced, "Sir, I'm getting worried. The LP is ten minutes late breaking squelch."

I told the soldier, "You break squelch on your radio and see if they respond." He did but the LP did not respond. I was contemplating speaking to them on the radio when Sergeant Adams said, "Sir, I got a better idea." He picked up an M-79 grenade launcher from a bunker, loaded it, aimed in the general direction of the LP and then fired a single 40mm round. A split second after the grenade went off, the LP radio broke squelch wildly. The next morning when those guys came in, Jim Nix, a big guy and a truly excellent soldier, had a vertical slice right in the center of the tip of his nose. (Good shootin,' Bruce!).

It's a fact of life that soldiers can sleep anywhere, even in situations where they might never wake up.

                                    ****

It was almost November and we were now off LZ Rita and working in a designated company AO. The 0700 Charlie Alpha was uneventful. Our job now was to search for and destroy the enemy within the boundaries of our company AO. To track the NVA, we searched for signs of movement on the many trails we encountered.

On my first night in the bushes with Delta Company, we selected an ambush site that was a straight piece of trail and we used the Delta 'bush. That night was to be the maiden voyage of the new Delta Company and our reign of terror against the NVA. We didn't dig holes to avoid making any noise. The platoon on the ambush was close enough to the trail to clearly see the entire length of the kill zone but not close enough that we would take casualties from our own grenades. There was no trip wire in the center of my ambush and there never would be.

For reasons I kept to myself, I selected White Skull and Lieutenant Doug Magruder to do my first ambush. Claymores were put out closer to the trail and covered with grass and weeds to hide them from view. The White Skull troops unhooked grenades from their web gear and laid them in front of them. On the ambush, half the guys could catch a catnap and the other half would watch the trail and the guys sleeping. Everyone was also responsible to stop any sound that might come from their napping comrades. In reality, I don't think anyone sleeps while on an ambush.

The idea of the full company doing an ambush, I know, must sound crazy to those who never tried it, but the tradeoff for the guys—the element of surprise and safety in numbers versus blindly running, scared shitless for friendly lines after doing a small ambush—made them successful. How many times, I wondered, had petrified soldiers out on a small ambush silently let the enemy walk by without trying to stop them. They feared if they didn't get killed by a much larger enemy force counter attacking, they'd surely get killed by their fellow soldiers trying to get back into the company perimeter.

As it turned out we had no customers on our first ambush, but we did have a little action the next day. In the morning after the non-ambush, I called each platoon leader and asked for a SITREP. Magruder confirmed all was well with White Skull. Johnson reported no problems with Rifle Range. Armstrong gave me, "Everything's okay, out!" I dropped my handset and launched myself in his direction. When I saw him, he still had his handset in his hand. In very unofficer-like terms I said, "Listen up, wise ass, you don't give me 'out,' I give you 'out!' When we get back to battalion I'm going to see about getting you out of Delta Company. Your attitude stinks." Perhaps he wasn't impressed because after I said my piece, he still had that smirk on his face that made me dislike him in the first place. Having threatened to run Armstrong out of the company, I began to wonder whether or not Colonel Henry would support me on this.

****

We stayed in the field beyond the middle of November. We had a couple of successful ambushes that produced several dead NVA bodies, some AKs, and some personal papers, which may have been of some value to the intel guys. Within a day or two of our successful ambushes, we also encountered the enemy head on as he was looking for us just as we were looking for him. These "meeting engagements," as the *Field Manual* calls these unexpected encounters, involve two forces on the move running into each other and reacting violently. The first troops from either side who realize they found the enemy open up and the other side quickly does the same. I immediately get on the radio requesting Army air support. *If we're taking more incoming fire than we're putting out, we can try to disengage and get some cover. The platoons on the flanks will start to link up behind the CP and begin making a perimeter so we can't be outflanked. The troops in front of the CP will spread out to get more firepower down range and attempt to link up with the other platoons behind the CP to complete the defensive perimeter so we can't be outflanked.*

The first thing I always call for in a tight fight is air support in the form of Army helicopters, either Cobras, armed Hueys or the

Light Observation Helicopter (LOH, nicknamed "Loach"). Nothing can get in closer quicker than armed helicopters. The enemy we met on the move was usually too close for either artillery or Air Force support to be effective without possibly killing us. Once the gunships arrive, the enemy usually begins his disappearing act.

I lost my first soldier KIA in the meeting engagement on November 18, 1968. He was Michael John Cromie from Harper Woods, Michigan. He was killed by rocket propelled grenade (RPG) fragments. He was twenty years old and is remembered on Panel 38 West, Line 6 of the Vietnam Wall.

After Michael was killed, it was again our turn to pull perimeter defense on the LZ. All fire bases in our area of operations were subject to mortar attack or, for that matter, human wave attack. Still, the troops felt safer on the LZ, sleeping in or near their bunkers, which were substantially built into the base perimeter. They were big enough for two men and had strong overhead cover consisting of steel planking and sandbags. They were also staggered along the perimeter so the bunkers could cover each other.

Delta's next casualty under my command occurred on November 26th on LZ Rita. This casualty was Raymond Joseph Ahern, Jr., of Philadelphia, Pennsylvania. Ray was the Radio Telephone Operator (RTO) for the artillery Forward Observer (FO) assigned to duty with Delta Company. Both the FO, who survived, and Ray were members of the 19th Artillery Regiment of the 1st Cavalry Division. The following tribute to Ray is posted on the Virtual Wall:

> *22 November 2005*
> *I remember Ray as someone I just clicked with. Every now and then you meet someone like that. He had an infectious smile and a warm way about him. We were both Irish Catholic kids from the Northeast and he was very easy to talk to. It was like being with*

someone from my neighborhood back home and after a few weeks I felt like I had known him for years.

We first met up north when we were working the Quang Tri area. In late October 1968 our division moved down into the area northwest of Saigon that borders Cambodia. It was a very different war than what we had seen in the Quang Tri area. We were no longer near villages and civilians. We were working in triple canopy jungle. We were running into large concentrations of North Vietnamese regulars who were well armed and liked to stay and fight.

One of the worst fire bases in our early days down south was LZ Rita. It was a very bad place from the first moment we stepped off the choppers. We had taken over from the 1st Infantry Division (Big Red One) on November 9th. They had been overrun the night before we got there. We stayed on Rita for several days to rebuild the bunkers and secure the area around the LZ. The bad guys were constantly hitting us with mortars and rockets and they were constantly probing our perimeter.

We then left the LZ and went out into the jungle about ten kilometers and started to sweep in a very large circle around the LZ. We conducted operations out in the bush for about ten days and were then sent back to defend the perimeter on Rita.

Ray was killed in the middle of the night on November 26, 1968 on Landing Zone Rita. His bunker took a direct hit from a rocket and he was killed instantly. I remember having to move out the next morning and it didn't seem right. There was no time to grieve or think about Ray or what had just happened, just move out and watch out for the bad guys.

He was a bright star in a very dark period in my life.
He made life in Vietnam a little more bearable for me
and I hope I did the same for him.

From a friend
Larry Hackett
Range One

Larry Hackett was one of my soldiers assigned to Rifle Range Platoon. After the war we met several times at the Wall on Veterans Day when he came to D. C. with a group of brothers to honor our fallen comrades. The last time I met with the guys who usually came to town with Larry, I was told that he had died of cancer. Ray Ahern was twenty years old at the time of death and is remembered on Panel 38W, Line 63 of the Vietnam Wall. Considering the high concentrations of Agent Orange defoliant we all walked through every day, one has to wonder if Larry Hackett's name shouldn't also be on the Wall.

We were to leave LZ Rita again the morning after Ray Ahern was killed but there was one matter I needed to take care of before we left, and I did that. Colonel Henry was apparently satisfied that he had a competent Delta Company commander, and he supported my request to get Lieutenant Armstrong out of my company. A new lieutenant had just arrived on the LZ, not yet assigned to a company. Colonel Henry told me, "Your replacement for Wild Cat platoon leader is Second Lieutenant David Spingath who just got here. I was going to send him out with you OJT but you can take him for keeps and leave Armstrong with me." I couldn't have been happier that the boss backed me on this, especially since I so publicly announced I was going to get rid of Armstrong. Dave remained with Delta Company as Wild Cat platoon leader for the remainder of my assignment as Angry Skipper 6.

Over the next several days, we continued to search during the day and lie in ambush at night and killed several more NVA without taking any casualties. It was clear that the men liked the company-size ambushes, and they were getting good at it.

****

On our next resupply day I was in for a surprise. As the resupply bird touched down, the artillery FO who had been with me since I took command of the company approached and told me he was being replaced and was leaving on the resupply chopper. He was a young buck sergeant (E-5) and, although I knew the FO position called for a lieutenant, I was satisfied with the sergeant's performance. I wondered why I wasn't in on any discussion about changing FOs but quickly realized this was a Division Artillery personnel decision and my input wasn't required. My new FO stepped off the resupply bird as the old one got on.

Lieutenant Jon Jones looked like cherub. He had rosy red cheeks, sparkling white teeth, curly blond hair and was, in my opinion, a little overweight. When he talked, he smiled. I didn't like him at all. He introduced himself to me and I said, "Jones, you'll travel in my CP. We ambush almost every night and every night when we stop moving we plot defensive targets (DTs). These must be precise so I hope you can read a map."

"Sir," he replied with a big toothy smile on his face, "you'll find that I am probably one of the best map readers in your company."

My answer to that was, "I think you will find out that I am the best map reader in Delta Company." With a twinkle in his eye and that same damn smile, he said, "We'll see, sir."

The first time we set up for an ambush after Jones joined the company, I showed him on the map where I wanted the DTs registered. He plucked the grid coordinates off his map and called them in to the Artillery Fire Direction Center (FDC) and almost immediately, an artillery round slammed into the earth a little closer than I thought it should have. I yelled at Jones, "Was that ours or theirs?"

"Yes," replied Jones.

"Yes what," I demanded.

"Yes, sir," answered Jones.

Well, we sorted it out and the round was ours. Since we used DTs as a reference point to redirect fire from, it was a good enough spot. Other DTs were registered without incident. As time passed, I got to like "Jonsey." Actually, it was pretty hard not to like him.

In the continuing course of our searching and destroying, I now found good reason to pay attention to Lieutenant Johnson. While moving through thick jungle with three columns abreast, we entered a large clearing where I caught a glimpse of Lieutenant Johnson in the column to my right. I noticed that he was walking behind his RTO rather than in front of him. That evening when we stopped to set up our perimeter and ambush, I asked him, "I saw you walking behind your RTO. Why are you doing that?" "Well, Skipper," he stammered, I can hear the radio better from behind him."

A totally bullshit reply. We didn't use speakers on our radios in the field. The only one who is supposed to hear the radio at all times is the RTO. If the call is for his boss, the RTO hands him the handset. I then asked Johnson, "Are you sure it's not because you heard that the sniper looks for the radio antenna and then shoots the man in front of it?"

"Oh no, Skipper, no way. I'm just more comfortable that way."

I replied, "I think the man you have walking in front of the radio now will feel more comfortable if you put yourself back in front of the antenna. Do it!"

Our ambush that night paid off with several dead enemy, some weapons and a map. As we were packing up to move out, my RTO told me Stone Mountain 6 wanted to talk to me. I took the handset and Mountain 6 advised, "Skipper 6, we need you to find a suitable

LZ ASAP. Charlie Company has gotten into it with a sizeable enemy force northwest of Rita and we're going to insert you into the fight, grid coordinates are XT 642883. The LZ we're going to insert Delta Company into is about a kilometer and a half from where Charlie is in contact. How long before you ID an LZ for extraction?" I quickly checked my map to get the coordinates of the large open space where I had observed Lieutenant Johnson walking behind his RTO. "Six," I said into the handset, "we can be ready for pick up in thirty minutes to forty-five minutes. How many choppers will be picking us up?"

"Can your LZ handle six slicks?" he asked.

I replied, "They have to stagger where they land but I'll have my guys assemble where each chopper should put down. It's going to take two lifts to get us all out. Will we have any overhead cover while the extraction is in progress?"

"Roger that," said the colonel. "You'll have some Blue Max Aerial Rocket Artillery (ARA) plus my Charlie Charlie to cover your extraction."

"Roger, 6. We are moving to the extraction LZ at this time."

In the clearing, I had six groups of ten soldiers take positions where the first six choppers could land. The rest of the company formed a protective perimeter which would shrink by half the company strength after the first lift out. My position on a normal extraction from the field was usually on the last lift out but this time, since we were apparently going from the frying pan into the fire, I would be going out with the first lift. Despite the dangers involved in dropping off the first chopper load of soldiers, or lifting out the last chopper load of soldiers, the operation was completed without incident. I had the grid coordinates of our destination and we proceeded forward to get into the fight.

While I was extremely sorry for the loss of two of my men, I was very pleased with the performance of the troops and my performance as CO. In the movie "Saving Private Ryan" Tom Hanks tells his troops that a commander has to believe he has made the right decisions even if some of his people are killed or wounded. He must believe if he had made different decisions, maybe more of his people might have been killed or wounded.

Nine

Chicken Valley

ONCE WE WERE ALL DROPPED OFF, ASSEMBLED AND moving towards the day's hottest battle in our AO, Colonel Henry in the Charlie Charlie gave me an azimuth and said he would guide us from above to ensure a safe link up with Charlie Company. Linking up two friendly units can also be a dangerous thing, especially if one of them is already in a fight. From a kilometer or so away, we could clearly see and hear the sights and sounds of the battle up ahead. Explosions, small arms fire, artillery and the sounds of Spooky, a modified USAF C-130 equipped with assorted canons and an M134 six-barreled Gatling-type minigun. The sound made by the side mounted Gatling is like a long continuous belch as it disgorges 7.62x51mm rounds at speeds of up to 6000 rounds-a-minute, surgically accurate and able to kill enemy within mere feet away from friendlies. The only thing more impressive than seeing Spooky working its sophisticated weaponry in the daytime is watching it at night. Going along with that endless belch of gunfire is a beautiful orange-red continuously solid line from the airplane to the ground caused by the tracer ammunition. That colorful line breaks only when the gunner takes his finger off the trigger.

In addition to Spooky, we could also see Blue Max Cobra gunships and assorted armed Hueys and Loaches flying above gray clouds of smoke. Adding to the scary scene was the sight of a disabled Cobra gunship wobbling and smoking as it passed low and slow over our heads and then fell out of the sky somewhere between us and the action in front of us. Colonel Henry advised that the Cav aviation battalion was already scrambling to rescue the crew and possibly recover the Cobra. He said they would be at the scene shortly so we should continue our march to link up with Charlie Company.

Unbeknownst to me, on our march toward this link-up, several of my men saw live chickens scurrying out of our way and into the bushes. From that sighting forward, to include reliving this operation in future D 2/8 reunions, this place will forever be known as "Chicken Valley."

Colonel Henry relied on Delta Company popping colored smoke and Charlie doing the same so he could tell from the air how close we were getting to each other. Finally my lead elements and men from Charlie Company were in contact. Since the enemy and Charlie were pretty much squared on each other, Delta was more on the enemy's right flank. Now Charlie, Delta and the enemy were in very close proximity to each other with the advantage going to the enemy due to their snipers in trees and the rest of them being able to shoot from bunkers and holes in the ground.

Shooting and grenade throwing became fast and furious. SITREPS from Doug Magruder told me that White Skull was now in contact with the NVA and at least one of his guys was already wounded. I told Doug to pop smoke. From the Charlie

Charlie, Colonel Henry, who heard the radio transmission and saw White Skull's smoke, said, "I identify goofy grape," (purple). Doug confirmed that his smoke was, in fact, "goofy grape." I asked, "How far in front of that smoke do you want the ARA?" Doug replied, "Twenty-five meters due north of the smoke." Colonel Henry also heard that transmission and he advised Blue Max where to shoot. Immediately, close-in machinegun fire and rockets poured into the area twenty-five meters in front of the smoke.

The procedure when using smoke to identify your position to friendly aircraft is to choose your color smoke grenade, deploy it and let the incoming aircraft, or Forward Air Controller (FAC) directing USAF air support, identify the color. If you popped green smoke and the incoming friendly aircraft or FAC identifies purple, that means the enemy is also using smoke grenades and monitoring our radio transmissions. If the situation arises where you pop one color smoke, and the friendly aircraft identifies another, instruct the pilot to turn away and not to descend towards the bogus smoke.

The fire from Blue Max Cobras in response to Doug's smoke had a decidedly positive effect for White Skull. After what seemed like a couple of hours of deadly combat, which was actually about forty-five minutes, contact between the NVA and Charlie and Delta Companies was beginning to peter out. The White Skull WIA was not serious and did not require immediate evacuation.

With a steel curtain of death coming down on the foe from the air and a blanket of heavy artillery behind the air cover designed to catch any fleeing North Vietnamese who may have escaped death by chopper, how could they again disappear? So many years after the war ended, we all know the answer to that question: Tunnels and mazes of tunnel networks. The intricate and numerous VC and NVA tunnels and systems which our enemy started digging, apparently during their war with the French, will be featured years from the date of this action on the History Channel show "Modern Marvels." Today they are even a tourist attraction in the south of the now unified Peoples' Republic.

Now the task at hand was to find, treat and medevac our wounded; count enemy bodies; and begin collecting weapons, equipment and documents. Charlie and Delta had formed a defensive perimeter. That word "perimeter" has probably been the most frequently used word so far in this story, but there was no front line in Vietnam and circling the wagons, a 360 degree defense, was the only way to stay alive. If the need arose for us to go outside our perimeter to do any of the previously described tasks, it would be done by heavily armed groups of men watching each other's back.

Delta had four men wounded, including Lieutenant Magruder. Doug left the field of battle in a medevac chopper but returned after medical treatment and a brief period of in-country convalescence. But this date, December 4, 1968, would become the worst day in my life because in this relatively brief encounter, Delta suffered three combat deaths. Years later, I am still sick over that day.

As the action slowed, it was soldiers from Charlie Company who reported that a group of NVA they had under observation appeared to want to surrender. Captain Gonzales further said, on the battalion radio net to Stone Mountain 6, that members of Delta Company's White Skull platoon were closest to these potential prisoners of war and suggested Delta Company close in on them. *Chieu Hoi* was the term in Vietnamese for surrendering, and it was always considered that live prisoners, as opposed to dead soldiers, were a valuable source of intelligence. I was not in a position to observe what was going on in this patch of jungle where some NVA allegedly wanted to surrender, but I urged my soldiers to use extreme caution in

The author as a young lieutenant newly assigned to RVN Airborne Brigade advisory detachment, July 1965

Soldiers of White Skull Platoon on LZ Rita, 1968 or '69

Soldiers of Wild Cat Platoon on LZ Rita, 1968 or '69

The author (*far left*) with platoon leaders (*left to right*) Bob Babas (Rifle Range 6), Dave Spingath (Wild Cat 6), and Preston Karr (White Skull 6)

Author (*right*) plotting next destination on a map while Radio Telephone Operator (RTO) Ray Haley opens a can of C-Rations

Gravesite of Corporal Warren Eskridge of Tangier Island, Virginia. Warren was the only soldier from Tangier to die in the Vietnam War. The wreath to the right of the grave was placed there by the author, Ed Regan and Mike McGhie of D 2/8

approaching them. But the NVA Charlie Company thought wanted to give up actually only wanted to kill some more Americans. By the time their true intentions were clear, three of my men were killed and, of course, so was the entire group of NVA that killed them. Delta dead in that tangle of jungle, bunkers and tunnels included:

Name	Age	Hometown	Wall Panel/Line
Donald Robert Stoltz	20	Milwaukee, WI	37W/42
Willie Gerald Jones	21	Fort Lauderdale, FL	37W/40
William C. Williams	22	Morton, MS	37W44

If I had said over the radio, rather than approach these potential POWs, "Just kill them," my guys might still be alive, but I think I would have a Uniform Code of Military Justice (UCMJ) problem, especially with Charlie Company insisting they wanted to give up. I really couldn't wait until our joint drill with Charlie Company was over. But it wasn't yet.

Delta and Charlie were now moving into a two-company perimeter encircling the members of these companies who were still searching for the wounded and, in our case, recovering the dead. We set up an LZ well inside the perimeter for medical evacuation and this LZ would also accommodate the arrival of brigade and division commanders and staff, and assorted intelligence types who will be arriving at the battleground, licking their chops at thoughts of perhaps finding maps and documents that would result in us being able to kill more and more VC and NVA.

Colonel Henry advised me that we may even have just found the elusive COSVN Headquarters. COSVN stood for the enemy's Central Office for South Vietnam, the main operational headquarters for the entire war in South Vietnam. If we were, in fact, standing on COSVN turf, the intel guys were going to uncover a treasure trove of VC and NVA plans. Appropriately,

Colonel Henry advised Captain Gonzales and me to plan to spend at least one more night in this location. There were too many bunkers to search and too many maps and documents to be gathered before darkness. The early warning about spending the night was much appreciated because now we had foxholes to dig, barbed wire to bring in and string, and sand bags to fill. The wire and bags, along with more ammunition, would be coming in ASAP on a resupply chopper. A counter attack overnight was just about guaranteed.

While Jon Jones and I plotted DTs around our portion of the perimeter, we coordinated with Charlie Company to ensure they were doing the same around their half of the circle. The scene inside the perimeter was a happy one. The brass felt we may really have had found the COSVN location and all the intel guys were drooling over marked up maps and written orders they were bringing out of bunkers by the bag full. Of course, all these people would fly out of there before dark and leave Delta and Charlie Companies to handle the expected counter attack. That, however, was as it should be.

Once the foxholes were dug, and then dug deeper, concertina wire was strung, gun emplacements were established and sand bagged and Claymore mines were set out and covered with brush, I had time to reflect on my three dead troopers. The friendly body count on my watch was now five and I'd had the company in the field less than two months. But, although every friendly loss is tragic, it was getting tougher on me because I was getting to know the men personally. Sergeant Williams, for example, was the squared away squad leader who asked me about being reassigned to the rear. He was the one with a wife, a son and a college degree and a bright future. His wife was now a widow, his son was fatherless, his college degree was worthless and his bright future was no longer a possibility. The loss of these three troopers as well as the two previously killed men was painful to me, as well as to all the friends they had made in the company. I knew their names now and could connect those names with faces. I didn't suffer the embarrassment I did after my first D Company KIA. After Michael John Cromie was killed on November 18th, I asked his platoon leader, "Where's Trooper Cromie been, R & R? I don't think I've seen him for a couple of weeks now." To which the lieutenant replied, "He's been dead for a couple of weeks now."

As I believe I said earlier, in this war, in this jungle, with this enemy, it was sheer insanity to believe that everyone is getting out of here alive.

****

All the battalion, brigade and division commanders, staff and intelligence personnel had been lifted out of "Chicken Valley." There was plenty of air cover overhead during their departure to ensure we didn't lose any VIPs. Double checking the perimeter, I was satisfied that foxholes were dug deep, wire was adequately strung and sand bags were filled and placed around fighting positions. The over two-hundred men of Delta and Charlie Companies accomplished a lot in a short amount of time, as if their lives depended on it, which really was the case.

By early evening, all the troops were watching the jungle in front of them, all of them knowing what was coming at us. I did not put out any word modifying the rules for some catching a few winks while others stayed awake, but I really didn't think that was necessary. I believed the night would be a 100% awake night.

Scary, Creepy and Deadly were not the names of three of the seven dwarfs but were words that accurately described our environment. That evening I hosted the battalion Catholic chaplain in my CP. He came in with the mob who descended on us earlier and, I believe, he either missed the last chopper out or just wanted to be with the soldiers. I thought, *If we don't get too busy tonight, I might tell him about my experience as an altar boy in Hawaii.* I walked the D Company portion of the perimeter talking to the troops, telling them artillery DTs were plotted, and in the event of a major million man counterattack, we would again have the services of Spooky, Blue Max and a host of others. I talked with Captain Gonzales and we were both satisfied we were ready for anything. I advised the chaplain that, in the likely event that we got incoming rockets and mortars, he was welcome to join me in my CP foxhole.

At some point after dark, that likely event began. Coming from any number of directions we all heard the unmistakable sound of enemy mortar rounds leaving the mortar tubes: *Whump, whump, whump* times forty. All this shit was in the air and coming our way! Anyone who did not have his steel pot on put it on ASAP and then got real small down deep in their foxholes. Me, my two radio operators, my artillery FO and his radio operator and the chaplain all jumped into the CP foxhole, and we all landed on top of Lieutenant Johnson lying on the bottom. I said, "Johnson, what the hell are you doing here?"

"Skipper, I was just checking the perimeter when I heard the mortars going off," he answered, "so I jumped in."

"Johnson," I said as calmly as I could, "your sector of the perimeter is nowhere near here. I think probably Rifle Range is better off without you tonight anyway. Enjoy the fight with the six of us standing on top of you because no one is getting out of this hole to let you up."

Somehow, I think Johnson was quite content to be at the bottom of the foxhole. (Note to Colonel Henry: I have another lieutenant who needs a new home). By the time my unexpected encounter with Lieutenant Johnson was over, the mortar rounds were impacting quite accurately inside our perimeter. I reported the contact to battalion who said Blue Max and Spooky were scrambling. In the meantime, my FO began calling in our DTs. In the darkness, we heard whistles and bugles blowing. We were returning fire in all directions. I didn't hear any Claymores going off, yet and I was glad about that because they should be detonated only when we actually observe enemy soldiers in front of them.

I no sooner thought that when Cat 6 called and said the enemy was just outside his wire and was attempting to turn the Claymores around towards the perimeter. If they were successful, over 700 ball bearings would clear out a large swath of Wild Cat Platoon's defense. Each platoon had a Starlight scope which gave us a night vision capability the enemy did not have and it was very helpful between the parachute flares, which were now being liberally dropped and turning night into day. The immediate action drill when a bad guy is caught trying to turn the Claymore is to blow it causing the enemy attempting to turn it to, as the Asians say, "lose face." All of it.

By now choppers, Spooky, Blue Max and many others were on station. The attackers meant business, they really wanted to kill us. As a flare would start to burn out, the Infantrymen on the perimeter could see stacks of bodies in front of them lying on slick, bloody jungle vegetation, then darkness. When the next flare lit up, they would see a new fired-up horde of angry North Vietnamese with AK-47 rifles with fixed bayonets coming at them. A radio transmission from Doug Magruder to me said some enemy had gotten past the concertina wire and were attacking the foxholes. I directed Spooky to put some fire in front of Doug's position.

Now, if you have been paying attention, you should have noticed that I have referred to our enemy in accurate and politically correct terms all throughout this story, so far. On my first tour I referred to my adversary as The Enemy, The Viet Cong, Victor Charlie,

Charlie and Charles. On this current tour I have referred to my adversary as The Enemy, The North Vietnamese Army, the NVA, and The Communists. I could have also referred to them as the People's Army of Vietnam (PAVN) but I didn't care for that acronym. NVA, to me, was more descriptive. But there is one announcement that got American soldiers defending a perimeter in Vietnam really fired up, with nostrils flaring and adrenalin flowing. And I made that announcement on both the company and battalion radio nets: "GOOKS IN THE WIRE!"

The output of our fire increased dramatically after that and from this point forward, I will call a spade a spade when and where appropriate. Sunrise would be significant for both sides in this fight. Everyone inside the wire was praying for it and everyone outside the wire was dreading it. Wherever the gooks had penetrated the wire they were repelled, and the fight continued.

I was The Man as far as Delta Company was concerned. When the shit hit the fan the men depended on me to call on whomever I had to in order to keep them alive. If I abandoned my radio, picked up a rifle and joined them on the perimeter, there would be a loud, collective, "Oh Shit!" coming from the troops. They knew that as long as artillery was pounding the enemy into the ground, machinegun and rocket fire from above was shredding the enemy and the parachute flares were lighting up the darkness, I was doing my job. In that regard, I was doing more than my part in adding to the enemy body count. Still, when telling war stories in the future, I cannot honestly say that I stood on my side of the wire shooting gooks down on their side of the wire mere feet in front of me.

The assault continued. The chaplain, who had no duties to perform in this situation, looked scared. No one could tell what Lieutenant Johnson looked like. Suddenly, over the battalion net I heard a Blue Max Cobra pilot begging, "Request permission to break formation. I've got hundreds of gooks in the open."

Over the radio I heard permission being granted and I hoped and prayed that the pilot and his weapons systems guy would kill every stinking one of them. It seemed as though we'd been in this fight for hours and, this time. it really was for hours. By now, I was pretty confident that, except for some slight rupturing of the perimeter which we quickly remedied, we were holding firm. When it was finally over and before we started the body counting, we would certainly need more ammunition of all types and I hoped they were planning on getting some water to us because most everyone's canteen would certainly be empty. Nothing makes a soldier thirsty like a good firefight.

Finally we began to see the first traces of daylight on the horizon. Spooky had to break off for refueling but was returning on station. I'm sure during the night many of the Cobras and Huey gunships had to refuel, but I didn't recall hearing any radio transmissions about aircraft going down. As we had come to expect, with the daylight the enemy began to fade away. To foil our measurement of success, they would take with them as many of their dead as they could carry or drag away. Although the direct assault on our perimeter was subsiding, the area outside the wire would still be dangerous.

It was decided by brigade headquarters that we should be resupplied and have our dead and wounded soldiers lifted out before we began counting dead enemy. Fortunately, this time, we had no KIA to take out and, hard as it may be to believe, no seriously wounded. We were also advised that our body counting of the enemy need not be that detailed as brigade would make a realistic estimate of what this fight cost the NVA in terms of lives. And the reason for an abbreviated body count was that the higher ups had decided to conduct an Arclight on the ground as soon as C and D Companies were a safe distance away. Arclight is the code name for the dropping of bunches of 750 and 1000 pound bombs by a flight of B-52 Stratofortresses flying out of Guam or Thailand. A safe distance away meant really, really far away. In consideration of the fact these planes may have already been in the air, medical evacuation and resupply needed to happen quickly followed by a rapid departure of C and D Companies from the area. Intelligence had apparently gotten all the information they could mine from the base camp and the generals had determined they would turn the land into a moonscape. They also concluded that the bunker complex, as lucrative as it might have been with Intelligence, was not the elusive COSVN.

The evacuation of those who required medical attention and resupply of ammo, water and rations did go quickly, thanks to the secure LZ we built inside the perimeter to bring in and take out the earlier KIA and WIA and, of course, brigade and division bosses and intel types. Charlie and Delta Companies, on the other hand, were not going to be lifted out but were to walk out, maintaining security and briskly to different sets of grid coordinates provided each company commander by Stone Mountain 6. By late morning, December 5, 1968, C and D Companies were on the move. There was no objective designated for us at the end of our march, just get the hell out from under the Arclight.

As bad as the fight in Chicken Valley was, neither Delta nor Charlie Companies suffered any KIA because we were prepared. Daylight revealed a scene more appropriate for a Hollywood horror movie. Those unlucky gooks designated to slip up to the wire and turn the Claymores lost more than their faces. In fact I saw one body where the Claymore turner had only his face and a section of spine left hanging on the wire. He must have raised himself above the Claymore to do his work. *Sin Loi* (sorry about that).

A flight of six B-52s dropping their bombs from 30,000 feet can level an area in the jungle over half a mile wide by two miles long. Delta and Charlie needed to get two or three, preferably three miles away from ground zero to avoid any possible damage. Being inside a box one mile by three miles around that rectangle of destruction is considered "Danger Close." As instructed, the two companies that fought that communist hoard the night of December 4th and 5th did move quickly but they still felt the earth tremble when the bombs exploded.

The fact that no one slept the night before caused me to forget about an ambush for the night of December 6th and just find an easy piece of terrain to defend and stop early for the night. We still had to circle the wagons, maintain noise and light discipline but in shifts, people needed to rest. As we were moving away from ground zero and the site of our all night fight, we were also moving away from Cambodia, which was probably where our enemy would seek sanctuary.

Beginning the morning of December 7th, Pearl Harbor Day, we would again resume our search-and-destroy operations. As we got closer to Christmas, Colonel Henry would rotate all four companies on and off LZ Rita so everyone got a chance to receive goodie boxes from home and have the Army's version of a Christmas meal.

During our walk away from danger, I gave some thought to Lieutenant Johnson. Acting First Sergeant Adams wanted to ship him back to Rita on the first resupply bird landing at our location. I started to have second thoughts, not about keeping him, but about branding him a coward. There's no doubt in my mind that walking behind the radio antenna was cowardly but maybe Johnson had some good reason to be in the vicinity of the CP foxhole when he heard the mortars. Quite possibly, he wanted to piss in my foxhole for calling him out earlier about the radio antenna. Obviously, Rifle Range Platoon held its own in the battle without their lieutenant. I had Sergeant Adams talk with the platoon NCOs and they said Johnson was capable of passing along my instructions to them but he showed no initiative, no leadership ability and he inspired no one. I decided not to humiliate the man by sending him back on a chopper, something Colonel Henry might not approve of, but it was still my intention to leave him on Rita the next time we stepped off.

****

After our recent fight, some of the guys came up with a plan for a device that would make our firing of Claymore mines during ambushes more efficient. The device used to detonate the mine is called a clapper or a clacker. This device is a small plastic box with a lever on top. When a soldier presses the lever down, the clapper sends an electrical impulse over wire to the blasting caps inserted into the mine, which in turn detonates the C4 explosive and propels the hundreds of steel balls into the kill zone. The device we came up with was a simple half-inch thick plywood board long enough to hold six Claymore clappers. The board was bordered on the sides and back by quarter-inch thick strips of plywood forming walls sufficiently high to keep each clapper in its own slot on the half-inch board. Each clapper is separated from the next by quarter-inch strips of plywood that form their slot on the half-inch thick board. The finished product, with six Claymore clappers set on it, looks somewhat like a piano keyboard. When the ambush is sprung, the operator looks somewhat like he's playing the piano. Somewhat.

We were pleased with our development of this ambush aide and sent our sketch to Lieutenant Derums in the rear to have three made and sent back to us. Karl did his job and our clapper keyboards were sent out on our next resupply. We continued to be very productive in our ambushing as we turned North Vietnamese wives into widows. Oh, did that sound cruel? Think of it this way: Their husbands were out to turn American wives into widows, so there! Time passed quickly and soon it was Delta Company's turn to man the bunkers and do Christmas on Rita. I didn't mean to make light of the Army's version of a Christmas meal because, after months of C-Rats, the meal was delicious and much appreciated. Along with the meal, Division Headquarters also sent the division band to the various fire bases to play Christmas music. It wasn't the Bob Hope show, but the troops liked it. And a special treat was arranged for us by the Signal Corps geniuses from brigade headquarters. Like magic, using a standard military radio and a two-niner-two antenna, a Signal Corps sergeant, through an arrangement with some other communications geniuses remotely located from Rita, enabled soldiers to make telephone calls home and talk for a few minutes with a loved one. Not having a wife at that time, I actually spoke with my mother for a few minutes. The catch was, in order for the remotely located geniuses to do their switching thing, each party to the phone call, when they finished saying their part, had to say "over" just like talking on a military radio net. My mom, bless her heart, had a lot of trouble dealing with the "over" part.

Probably my best Christmas present was Colonel Henry agreeing to take Lieutenant Johnson off my hands in exchange for a newly arrived, green, second lieutenant. Fine by me. The new lieutenant's name was Bob Babas and, like Lieutenant Dave Spingath with Wild Cat, he would remain the Rifle Range platoon leader for the remainder of my term as CO. Colonel Henry screwed Lieutenant Johnson into a hole somewhere on the battalion staff and I felt sure that Johnson was pretty pleased with how things worked out.

A lot of guys did receive Christmas goodie boxes from home and the troops devoured homemade cookies and other treats, and everyone shared his Christmas delights with others from the company.

After our Christmas break, we departed Rita and went back to ambushing, killing and collecting weapons, maps and personal papers. Towards the end of the third week in January, it was again Delta's turn to man the bunkers at LZ Rita. But the soldiers would come to regret those Christmas goodie packages from home because, on our return to the bunkers, we found that cookie crumbs and other snack residue had sent out an invitation to rats the size of house cats to move in with the troops.

Then, on the night of January 21, 1969, a night which had up to this point been silent and uneventful, a single explosion in the middle of Rita lit everything up and caused additional explosions as it sympathetically set off mortar rounds stacked in our ammo pit. The troops were 100% awake after the explosions and ready for an attack, but it never came. The rest of the night was again silent. In the dark, platoons tried to get a head count to ensure everyone was alive, but we wouldn't be able to confirm this until daylight.

In the morning daylight, we found that all Delta Company troopers were present and accounted for. Then, while checking the perimeter of the LZ to ensure that the barbed wire and other physical barriers were intact, members of Wild Cat Platoon found an arm obviously recently blown off of its owner. We initiated a search looking for more parts. After peering beneath some steel planking, which was partially covering an ammo storage pit, Sergeant Terry Shoopman, the man who put Elliot Velez-Rodriguez on the perimeter the night before, became reacquainted with what was left of this unfortunate soldier.

Trooper Elliot Velez-Rodriguez was a replacement who was going to be assigned to A Company. He had arrived on Rita, however, while Alpha was in the field and Delta was doing LZ defense. Velez-Rodriguez probably would have gone out to Alpha Company on their next resupply chopper, maybe even the next day. But for that night, with another soldier and rifle on the LZ and Wild

Cat short of men, Cat squad leader Sergeant Shoopman used his initiative and inserted Trooper Velez-Rodriguez into the LZ defense. Rather than being *placed* into a body bag once found, this soldier's remains were scooped up and *poured* into a body bag. Years later, more than one Delta Company soldier exposed to this grizzly recovery, while putting together a claim for VA benefits for PTSD, asked me to write a "stressor" letter in support of his claim citing the trauma resulting from their participation in the incident that turned Trooper Velez-Rodriguez into jello. I was happy to do as they asked. The explosion that killed Trooper Velez-Rodriguez is still a mystery. Some think Elliot killed himself either accidently or on purpose. Others believe the enemy put a satchel charge on a bent over tree and launched it like a sling shot onto the LZ. Patrols out from Rita later that day did find evidence of enemy activity not too far outside the wire, which supported the satchel charge theory. The Army officially attributes the death of Specialist Fourth Class Elliott Velez-Rodriguez to "Artillery, rocket or mortar." He is remembered on Panel 34W, Line 54 on the Vietnam Wall. At first I thought that Trooper Velez-Rodriguez's death shouldn't be counted in the Delta Company body count on my watch because he wasn't officially in my company. I quickly realized, however, that this thought was total bullshit. Elliot died serving with D Company, doing a D Company job, while we were manning the perimeter of LZ Rita. He absolutely does count as a soldier who died on my watch and is included on the Honor Roll with the other KIA members of Delta Company, 2/8 Cavalry.

****

Before again leaving LZ Rita, Colonel Henry gave me the big picture as far as future operations were concerned. It seems we were to abandon Rita (Good riddance) and would be operating off Fire

Support Base Saint Barbara for a while. Saint Barbara was a very large base which used to be a French fort. It was actually in the 25th Infantry Division's ("Tropic Lightening") AO so our battalion would not be putting a company on perimeter security; troops from the 25th ID would do that. Colonel Henry would then have all four of his line companies out killing gooks at the same time and the enemy body count and weapons seized statistics for the battalion would presumably show a marked increase.

Artillery units from Corps level were situated on Saint Barbara and, in addition to 105mm and 155mm howitzers, the guns we usually relied on for artillery support, Saint Barbara boasted 175mm pieces and 8-inch guns. These big guns supported any friendly units within range to include the RVN, ROK and any other allies who needed their support. The LZ did not get its name from any previous commander whose wife who was named Barbara. Saint Barbara is the patron saint of the artillery and with its massive artillery capabilities, Saint Barbara was a true fire support base.

(Saint Barbara was also very close to Nui Ba Den, which all the U.S. soldiers translated as "Black Virgin Mountain." I, who took eight weeks of Vietnamese, knew that it literally translates as "Black Lady Mountain." Remember your language lesson from Chapter Five: "Ba" is a married woman; "Co" is an unmarried woman. But a quick check with Wikipedia on the Internet shows that the mountain is referred to, in the same article, as both "Black Lady Mountain" and "Black Virgin Mountain," so forget about my eight week language course and take your pick.)

The mountain sticks out because it is the only elevation on otherwise flat land. It is 3,268 feet high. It was widely said and believed that, although the Americans owned the top of the mountain, the VC and NVA owned the rest, including within the mountain which was honeycombed with tunnels (No shit!).

Saint Barbara would prove interesting but in the meantime, we still had some searching and destroying to do before saying goodbye to Rita. On the 28th of January, our searching paid off but our destroying was a little weak. As was probably inevitable, even though we walked with a three platoon front, we walked into a prepared enemy base camp and bad people were at home. We took heavy fire from the front and took some immediate casualties. I told the platoon leaders to attempt to disengage and get behind some cover. I also called for gunship support and advised Stone Mountain 6 we were in a fight. We were able to back up and the enemy didn't attempt to move forward with us, probably because they were firing from prepared foxholes and bunkers and were not ready to abandon their cover and take us on hand-to-hand. That provided some breathing room between them and us and made some space for the gunships to put some fire on them with less chance of hitting any of us.

Because this enemy was in trenches and, no doubt, had access to tunnels, they would have some protection from the gunship fire so I expected our fire fight to last a while, which it did. We stayed in contact throughout the rest of the day and then into the night. We had managed to form a tight perimeter and as darkness came we were reacquainted with Blue Max ARA and Spooky. We also scraped out some shallow fighting positions to give us a little cover. The jungle was very thick where we were and I think that is the reason we weren't receiving mortar or RPG fire. Some time prior to leaving Rita, everyone was issued a small orange in color strobe light which became very useful at night lighting up our perimeter for Spooky and Blue Max to see. Parachute flares used in great quantity during the Chicken Valley fight were not desirable in this fight since they would be lighting us up for the enemy as we were substantially above ground rather than in foxholes. We also managed to move our wounded off the line and inside the perimeter.

During the night the NVA attempted several probes at various points of our defense but we did not allow them to get in. Throughout the night some of the wounded moaned or screamed and I wished there was more we could do for them. As it was, we were still in a fight and the company medics were doing all they could. Daylight couldn't have come any sooner and the enemy did his usual disappearing act. We blew a one ship landing zone in the middle of our perimeter to get resupplied and get the wounded and dead out. We had two troopers killed and several wounded. The dead were Warren Eskridge from Tangier, Virginia, and Carl Pipher from Canton, Ohio. Warren was twenty-one years old at the time of his death and is remembered on Panel 33 West, Line 7 of The Wall. Carl was twenty years old and is remembered on the Wall on Panel 33 West, Line 11.

Years later during a Veterans Day 1st Cavalry reunion in Washington D.C., myself and two other Angry Skipper guys drove to Crisfield, Maryland, and hitched a ride on the boat that brings mail and supplies to Tangier Island in the Chesapeake Bay. We went there to meet the family of Warren Eskridge, the only soldier from Tangier Island to die in the Vietnam War. We had prearranged this visit by email and phone calls. Warren's sisters had found the Angry Skipper website a few years earlier and had been communicating with some of the guys for a while.

We had invited them to be honored guests at any of our reunions but they never came. The other two troopers and I got quite choked up when, as the boat neared the dock at Tangier Island, it appeared that the entire population of the island was standing on the pier waiting for us. And, in addition to Old Glory flying from a flagpole on the dock, just below it was the yellow and black flag of the 1st Cavalry Division.

After laying a wreath, which we had made and brought with us at Warren's grave, we went to one of the sister's houses for "fellowship" as she called it, and we discussed Warren. We met

Warren's twin brother and, at the time of our visit, he was the mayor of Tangier Island. Then, one of the sisters produced the letter she said I had written to her parents about Warren's death. I held my breath knowing I never did write such a letter. When she showed it to me, I saw it wasn't signed but was written over my signature block. Of course, it would have been Karl Derums who wrote the letter, not me. I should have worked this out with Karl right after I took command, but that didn't occur to me at the time. I would have told Karl that he was writing on my behalf and to sign the damn letter himself. I held my breath as I read the letter and I wished that Karl had been in the same room, so I could kill him. The letter said Warren was killed when we, "… walked into an ambush."

We never walked into an ambush! We either encountered the enemy head-on while looking for him or we were killing him when he walked into our ambush. If I had been anywhere else except the family home of one of my KIA soldiers, I would have flipped out.

Warren Eskridge was indeed an individual beloved by his family and I was pleased to meet them. In the face of this fucking letter, however, I could do nothing but sit there and look remorseful. We stayed overnight at a bed and breakfast on the island. That night, as I tried to go to sleep, precisely because Warren was so beloved and he died under my command "walking into an ambush," I had visions of that same population of Tangier Island that we saw on the pier, walking as a mob, complete with torches and pitch forks, to this bed and breakfast, to string me up.

Ten

Homeless on Saint Barbara

T HE 2D BATTALION, 8TH CAVALRY REGIMENT had no LZ to
call home. All four rifle companies were basically homeless
and left to wander in the jungle, not necessarily aimlessly, in
order to meet new people and kill them. Not having an LZ is not
really a bad thing when you consider that one third of the soldiers
of Delta Company that had been killed on my watch died taking
a direct rocket or mortar hit while on LZ Rita. But, while we
were out searching and destroying, changes were taking place.

Lieutenant Colonel Frank Henry, quite frankly, the best boss I
ever had in the military, was suddenly gone. He was transferred
elsewhere and, when we again stepped on LZ Saint Barbara, I
would meet the new Stone Mountain 6, Lieutenant Colonel
Richard Wood. I may have gotten a radio call from battalion
telling me that Frank Henry was leaving, but I can't recall if I did
or not. It's like Larry Hackett said in his tribute to Ray Ahern on
the virtual wall, something happens and a good friend is gone but
we just "move out and watch out for the bad guys." Of my seven

months in command, I worked for Colonel Henry for four and a half of those months and he rewarded me for my work with a terrific Officer Efficiency Report (OER), rating me number one out of his five company commanders and stating, "CPT Colavita and his company have been constantly in the thick of every firefight encountered by this battalion. During one battle, CPT Colavita's company and one other from this battalion stood off three sustained attacks supported by heavy mortar and RPG fire. The results were over forty enemy KIA by body count and no friendly personnel killed. This is a good example of the consistently outstanding performance by CPT Colavita and his men." The battle mentioned is, of course, "Chicken Valley."

Lieutenant Colonel Richard Wood, the new Stone Mountain 6, didn't wait for his companies to come onto Saint Barbara to meet them. The colonel and his S-3, Major James Bramlett, got on the Charlie Charlie and flew into the bushes to meet us. Colonel Wood struck me as a capable and competent boss, and, as I would learn over forty years later when we met as civilians for the first of many lunches together and dinners with our wives, a nice guy and a real gentleman. But, I had grown used to hearing Colonel Henry's comforting voice over the radio, particularly when we were fighting for our lives, and I would miss it. After meeting Colonel Wood, I was sure I'd have the same relationship with him as I had with Colonel Henry.

LZ Saint Barbara was just one of an annoying string of fire bases strung along the Cambodian border. Annoying to the enemy, of course. These fire bases were all within 105 mm Howitzer range of at least one other firebase so they could support each other with artillery in case of an NVA attack. The enemy did not have a logistical tail keeping the attacking forces resupplied from the rear. Rather, the job of the communist logisticians was to preposition supplies in strategic locations in front of the main forces, so when they reached a position from which to attack a firebase, city, province or anything else, everything they needed would be there waiting for them. That's why these fire bases were annoying. The NVA logisticians moving supplies forward were often the ones getting caught and being killed in American ambushes with the resulting loss of whatever they were trying to preposition. The 1st Cav built, operated from and then abandoned fire bases as needed, depending on what Intelligence believed the enemy was doing. When the enemy had lost an intolerable amount of logisticians, weapons, ammunition, and rice, that's when they would attempt to take out one of these fire bases with an overwhelming attacking force.

We operated off LZ Saint Barbara during the month of February and most of March 1969. On my first Vietnam tour, the enemy was primarily Viet Cong guerrillas from the south. Our primary enemy now in the War Zone C portion of the III CTZ, was well trained and equipped NVA soldiers. There were still Viet Cong divisions in the enemy's order of battle, but they had been rebuilt with fighters from the North following the VC's almost total annihilation during the infamous Tet Offensive of 1968.

While we did our search-and-destroy operations in our portion of War Zone C, the woods were full of communist troops either trying to get supplies closer to Saigon, or already equipped main force units working their way south to disrupt America's resurrected pacification campaign in the populated areas. After General William Westmoreland's departure from Vietnam, his replacement, General Creighton Abrams, deemphasized the body count as the measure of success and placed new emphasis on pacification and winning support of the South Vietnamese people for their own government.

It was while we operated off Saint Barbara that the 1st Cavalry Division Headquarters began also annoying their own rifle company commanders in the field. Thinking back on these events, I have to wonder if it was some kind of test.

Without asking for it, I was advised by radio one day that we would be getting a tracker dog team, a German Shepherd and handler. I was told to find an LZ suitable to bring this team to my location and let them hook up with us. My understanding of the tracker dog team was that their specialty was following blood trails of wounded enemy troops in order to capture them. But we were not in the business of tracking down injured gooks. It was our job to kill them dead the first time. The dog thing pissed me off also because I am a major dog lover and the possibility of this big, beautiful German Shepherd getting hurt or killed with my company really disturbed me. The other thing contributing to my displeasure was that this dog had to be resupplied, at least every other day, with dog food. He apparently ate so much that his handler couldn't carry more than two days of food at a time. So much for my plan to go as far and as long as we could without resupply.

After several days, maybe even a week, Colonel Wood asked how the dog team was working out and I told him it was proving to be pretty worthless. On our next resupply day, the dog team boarded the chopper and left.

The next special team inflicted on us was a Psychological Operations (PsyOps) team. This consisted of one U.S. soldier, one Vietnamese military interpreter and a megaphone. Their job was to convince any enemy we encountered to surrender, or *Chieu Hoi*, as the Vietnamese say. This team didn't require any special food or cause us any particular difficulty, but for some reason or other, they never encountered any living enemy soldiers that they could convince to surrender. All the enemy we encountered either got away alive or stayed behind dead. After a while, they too boarded a resupply chopper and left.

The next and most obnoxious specialty was the Pathfinder. On his arrival, this corporal announced that he had been sent to

Delta Company to direct the landing and departure of any aircraft visiting our location, something I thought we were doing quite well without him. At least this clown didn't have to be resupplied every other day like the dog did, although I liked the dog much better.

Shortly after the arrival of our Pathfinder, we found a very busy trail with Ho Chi Minh sandal prints, NVA canvas shoe prints and bicycle tire prints all pretty fresh and going in both directions. Even though it was earlier in the day than usual for us to stop, this trail was too good to pass up. Since it appeared very possible that we could encounter a large body of enemy soldiers, I passed the word that we should dig holes to fight from if, after the ambush, the remainder of this force turns on us. With security out to the flanks and rear, the guys began digging foxholes as quietly as possible.

The Pathfinder was not digging. When I asked him why he wasn't digging he replied, "Pathfinders don't dig holes!" I then said to him, "Well, then you have a problem because Delta Company doesn't dig holes for Pathfinders." The last time I looked he was trying to borrow an entrenching tool.

This trail seemed very likely to be a perfect place for an ambush. I notified the TOC about the trail along with where we were on the map and advised that we would be calling in DTs. After dark, while sitting on this trail waiting for what should be a big kill, we were notified by radio to do what I thought was the dumbest thing I had ever heard of. Major Bramlett told me, "The G-3 believes the night still belongs to the NVA so we want you to pick up and move another kilometer or so, over." I could not believe what I'd just heard. We, Delta Company, had been killing gooks in the dark for months now, and killing them because they were moving and we were stationary. I replied to the major, "Three (nickname for an S-3 or G-3), we are sitting on a hot trail and I believe we have a great opportunity to kill a bunch of guys tonight. If we pick up and move we'll be vulnerable."

"Regardless," came his answer, "division wants all companies to move at night."

I thought about the old, "Say again, you're coming in broken and garbled," but everybody knows that one. So I said, "Three," we've got movement on the trail. Out!" In doing that, I remembered how mad I got when Lieutenant Armstrong had given me "out." But I did it and now I could only hope we did get some action. Fortunately, we did.

My personal belief is that I really never slept while we were off the LZ and ambushing. I say this because, even though I might appear to be dozing, my RTO never had to wake me up to answer a radio call. I always heard my own call sign coming over the radio even though the radio volume was set very low and the caller was whispering. But it wasn't the radio that got my attention this night. It was the sound of many Claymores going off in rapid succession. I could just see in my mind my troops hitting those clappers on our plywood keyboard.

After the Claymores stopped, we received no incoming fire. With a heavy cloud of smoke still hanging in the air, there was complete silence, except for the sound of falling trees. At that time, I had no idea what lay out there on the trail. After a long while, we began to hear some moaning coming from the trail, which was answered by a couple of grenades in the direction of the sound. After the grenades, the moaning stopped but then we heard the sound of more falling trees.

It was a dark, moonless night and I was not going to put any of my soldiers at risk by having someone step out to check the damage. We had already lost three guys in Chicken Valley attempting to take what appeared to be some willing prisoners. The next morning we had over a dozen dead, uniformed NVA soldiers on the trail. It wasn't easy to get a body count or to find the weapons and documents they were carrying because our liberal use of Claymores and grenades blew several trees and other jungle vegetation down on top of the deceased enemy and what they were carrying. Whatever this contingent of a dozen or so (actually 14) were up to, I believed we got everyone on the trail that night. There were no blood trails or drag marks indicating some might have been dragged or otherwise gotten away.

We called in our body and weapons counts and advised we would turn weapons and documents over on our resupply, which, I requested, to be today because, if nothing else, we needed new Claymores and grenades. The TOC called back with the coordinates of a nearby clearing which, I was advised, would be the site of our resupply. We were also advised that Mountain 6 and Mountain 3 would be visiting us in that LZ. I checked the clearing on my map and responded that we would be heading there ASAP. We all felt like we earned our money with that ambush, but we believe the enemy now knew where we were and we really had to be observant as we moved.

On our arrival at the clearing, we would need to recon the area and make sure we had it well secured for the visit of Stone Mountain 6 and 3. If it weren't for the need to restock up on Claymores and grenades, I would have tried to beg off this visit preferring to get miles away from the scene of the crime. The resupply was quickly accomplished and the visit of Stone Mountain 6 and 3 was a good thing. Colonel Wood congratulated us on an ambush well done and then we had a little impact award ceremony to hand out some medals that were earned during our last fight. For morale purposes, the 1st Cavalry Division started an impact award program designed to present awards to deserving troopers as soon as possible after the actions for which these awards were earned. As I was shown the list of those receiving medals, I radioed the platoon leaders and told them to round up their guys and bring them to my location. The colonel and the S-3 thanked these soldiers for their good work and shook their hands and my guys gave them a snappy salute. I was expecting something to be said about not moving at night, but I didn't hear anything about it. As for our Pathfinder, I can only assume he got on the chopper with the 6 and 3 because I never saw him again. If I recall correctly, the Pathfinder ended the stream of unwanted help.

I think the idea of the impact award program was good for morale but, unfortunately, the paperwork, that is the actual numbered orders authorizing these awards, failed to materialize in many cases. Years later at reunions, myself and company commanders before and after me, as well as platoon leaders, were often asked to write letters for our troops in support of their requests to the Board for Correction of Military Records that awards they earned, which were never made official, be added to their DD 214s. Form DD 214 is the document showing a soldier's separation from service as well as schools attended, achievements, promotions, awards and decorations. Mostly, these requests for medals earned but not officially awarded had a happy ending. It appeared over the years that the Board, with letters of support from former commanders and fellow soldiers, was properly giving these soldiers what they earned.

I had such a request for assistance by a former D Company NCO at the Angry Skipper reunion I hosted in Washington, D.C. in the summer of 2002. This former sergeant asked me to help him get a Bronze Star Medal (BSM) with "V" device (for Valor) and a Purple Heart. He told me that after he was wounded and on a medevac flight to the States, a brigadier general boarded the plane in Hawaii and began pinning Purple Heart medals on the patients who had been wounded, which was just about all of them. When he got to my former sergeant, before he had a chance to say anything, my former sergeant told me that he told the general, "You can take that fucking medal and shove it up your ass." The former sergeant then told me that the general replied, "Son, some day you are going to be sorry you said that." Well, that day had arrived. When he asked for my help, I said, "The general was right, wasn't he? I'll see what I can do."

Turns out, I couldn't do much as far as the BSM with "V" was concerned. I still had the notebook I carried in my left shirt pocket the entire time I was Angry Skipper 6 in which I wrote down almost everything that happened on a given day. I searched through my notebook and it did not contain anything about a BSM with "V" for this man. That doesn't necessarily mean he was lying about the medal because anyone in the company could put anyone else in for an award. Normally, it would pass through me on its way up the chain, but not necessarily. I may have been verbally informed that a platoon leader or platoon sergeant put so-and-so in for an award and that is something I may not have written down. Getting the names of those killed or wounded would have been a higher priority for me. And then, any awards from the field had to pass scrutiny by the battalion commander and the S-1, who might downgrade or reject an award for not meeting the necessary criteria. If it cleared battalion and went up to brigade, it would again be examined before going on to division, or not, where the division personnel people could approve, downgrade or reject it. At any of those levels, his BSM with "V" might have been rejected or downgraded.

I was trying to get a handle on the BSM before helping him with the Purple Heart, which we all knew he earned, but he screwed himself out of when he mouthed off to the general. When officers board a medevac aircraft to award Purple Hearts, an assistant is always along in order to get the names, ranks and serial numbers of the wounded to verify the award and then ensure orders are cut making the awards official. I always looked forward to Angry Skipper reunions but I really didn't look forward to meeting with this former sergeant because he was really expecting me to do something for him with this BSM and it wasn't going to happen. No one I talked to from the company could substantiate the medal he said he earned. Many years passed since he told the general to shove it so I felt he could wait a bit longer. But at a subsequent Angry Skipper reunion after he asked for my help, he was not among the attendees. I asked about him and was told he had died shortly after the last reunion.

****

Approaching the four month mark in my tenure as Angry Skipper 6, I felt I was really getting to know my soldiers. There was one real sharp buck sergeant in Wild Cat Platoon I came to notice. His last name was Goochie and he was always clean shaven with close cut blond hair, and was constantly giving life saving advice to the younger soldiers. On one search-and-destroy mission, I approached Sergeant Goochie as we walked through the bush and asked him if he had given any thought to a career in the Army as an officer. I gave him a sincere pitch about Officer Candidate School at Fort Benning. The sergeant replied that he appreciated the talk and said he would consider OCS. We were now into February and still stinging from our personnel losses of January 28th. We had no way of knowing that February 5th would be another one of those days. On February 4th, we set up our night ambush on the last piece of high ground before the earth sloped down to meet a creek and then again went up hill. There was a decent looking trail we could ambush on just before the trail started down the hill to the creek, which we knew from our maps was there. As usual our ambush paid off but only to the tune of one lone NVA.

In the morning we called in the kill to the TOC and secured the enemy's rifle and personal documents. Then we saddled up to proceed down the hill to the stream that we intended to cross and continue onward until it was time to set up the next night's ambush or, of course, until we met the enemy.

We met the enemy shortly after we started downhill. Intense fire came at us from a broad front across the creek. Our right column point man was immediately killed and other troops were wounded. I called Stone Mountain 6 asking for immediate gunship assistance. Without waiting for any order from me, my lead elements started backing up away from the enemy and everyone was firing their rifles and desperately looking for something to hide behind. There was precious little cover.

Most of the lead elements of the company were on this downhill slope and in the open, including my CP. Within minutes, I heard from incoming chopper pilots asking where we were in relation to the enemy. I told them we were all on the south side of the creek and the enemy was dug in on the north side. The gunships immediately went to work with machineguns and rockets giving the enemy something else to think about besides killing us. I had several men hit but most were still able to fight. Lieutenant Doug Magruder was again wounded but was still shooting. The point man who was killed, Chester Kmit of Williamsburg, Massachusetts, was shot dead in the first burst of fire. Unfortunately, he would be temporarily left behind but certainly not forgotten.

The fight raged on. Thanks to the gunships, we were able to back away towards higher ground and some trees and rocks to use for cover. When the enemy fire started to peter out we started collecting the wounded behind the crest of the hill. I could hardly believe it when I learned that only two soldiers were seriously wounded, one was Corporal James Edmonds and the other was the ever sharp-looking Sergeant James Goochie. Both of these men urgently needed medevac but it was still too dangerous to ask a medevac chopper to land. The other wounded, like Lieutenant Magruder, had been shot in non-life threatening places, one shoulder, two arms, three legs and one buttocks. They, to a man, wanted to wait for a more suitable and secure landing zone from which to be lifted out. Edmonds, however, was close to death and would die if not medevaced immediately, and Sergeant Goochie was not looking good. A deal was struck, I believe, between Stone Mountain 6 and a medevac chopper.

The chopper would fly low overhead and drop down a rigid litter. This was a stretcher in which Edmonds could be securely strapped. Then the chopper would hover high overhead and lower a jungle penetrator by a steel cable which we would connect to the stretcher. Trooper Edmonds would be hoisted up to the aircraft and brought into it. During the lift, the gunships would stay on station to suppress enemy fire.

Our medics strapped Edmonds into the rigid litter, the chopper lowered the penetrator, we connected the cable to the stretcher and Trooper Edmonds was immediately in the process of being lifted up by the helicopter. The penetrator cable was being wound up electrically as the chopper was gaining altitude so Edmonds was being hauled up fast. Then the enemy opened fire again and hit the helicopter. Suddenly, to my shock and horror, I saw the cable unwinding and Edmonds was plummeting to earth. Someone on the medevac chopper had cut the cable, no doubt in a panic over being shot at and hit. But Edmonds was clear of any trees or anything else to snag on and bring down the chopper. The cable did not have to be cut. I hoped Edmonds was not conscious when this occurred because, as he was strapped tightly into the rigid litter, his knees would be locked and as he hit the ground feet first, I imagined his shattered leg bones would be jammed upward into his body. If he wasn't dead before he hit the ground he certainly was after. Again, the gunships rained death down upon the enemy and we disengaged and moved back to last night's location.

There was a clearing near where we spent the previous night which was large enough for a single helicopter, but we had to blow down some trees in the middle of it. With the gunships keeping the NVA busy, we moved back to our proposed LZ. Immediately troops began wrapping the trees to be blown with det cord and chunks of C4 explosives. Everyone took cover. The soldier who was to send the electrical charge to the C4 started yelling the required "Fire in the hole!" three times. Then I looked around for Sergeant Goochie and saw that he was still lying on a stretcher in the middle of the clearing. As quickly I could, I ran towards the stretcher and threw myself on top of the man. Just before the C4 blew, Sergeant Goochie whispered in my ear and told me to do something very similar with OCS as a previously mentioned sergeant told a general to do with a Purple Heart medal. When the C4 exploded, a large piece of tree trunk slammed into my back knocking the wind out of me.

As guys came out from behind cover, it was clear that no one had seen the most heroic thing I had done in Vietnam. I got my wind back without anyone noticing anything. With a suitable LZ now ready, a different medevac ship landed in the LZ and picked up our KIA trooper, Sergeant Goochie, Lieutenant Magruder and half-a-dozen less seriously wounded soldiers.

Now it was time for a different helicopter to land and drop off more ammunition. Almost everything expended in this fight was 5.56 mm rifle ammo and 40 mm grenade rounds for the M-72 grenade launcher. When all this was done, we would be staying the night in last night's foxholes, only dug a little deeper.

First thing in the morning our job would be to recover the body of Chester Kmit. But, first thing the next morning, my mission became, "Stay in place." Mountain 6 called and told me that the commander of the medical unit that owned the medevac chopper that dropped Edmonds was conducting an investigation into the matter and he would be landing at our location some time during the day. We were to stay put until this interview was over. Depending on when the investigating officer arrived, we might have to spend an unheard of third night in this location and Trooper Kmit would be spending another night down by the creek. And that's the way it worked out. It was late afternoon before the investigating officer flew in to talk to us. We popped colored smoke for his chopper and guided it into the LZ. A Medical Service Corps colonel exited the chopper followed by several others.

As he introduced himself to me, I noticed that one of the members of his party was looking very nervous. I assumed this individual was the one who blew the cable dropping Trooper Edmonds to the ground. Several of us who saw the unraveling cable were interviewed. I stated that Trooper Edmonds was clear of the trees and the fact that he was tethered to the chopper presented no threat to the chopper. I have no idea if any of my men had any other opinions. I never heard anything about the findings of the investigation. I have come to realize that, since the medevac chopper did take several small arms hits, this could have easily scared that crew member into blowing the cable, and Trooper Edmonds, who was gravely wounded, may have expired before the cable incident even happened.

After the third night in this same location, it was morning and definitely time to recover the body of Trooper Kmit. But wait, as they say in TV commercials for the Pocket Fisherman, there's more. We were now told to stand by at our location for an incoming chopper carrying the returning First Sergeant Ramon

Cruz back from his re-enlistment leave. I advised the battalion RTO who gave me this news that the chopper carrying First Sergeant Cruz better hurry up because the whole company was upset about Trooper Kmit still lying by the creek. If the chopper hadn't been airborne as we spoke, I would have asked that Sergeant Cruz be delivered to us after we secured Trooper Kmit.

I then told Acting First Sergeant Adams to pack up his gear and get ready to return to Saint Barbara. Once on the LZ, he needed to get himself to the battalion rear where he could finish out the remaining few weeks of his tour in Vietnam. Karl Derums could find Adams something to do until his DEROS, but far as I was concerned, Sergeant First Class Adams had done a tremendous job for me as acting first sergeant and I felt it would be wrong to demote him back to platoon sergeant.

When the chopper arrived I said goodbye to SFC Adams and hello to First Sergeant Cruz. I had not seen the man since shortly after I took over the company and I would not be welcoming any input from him now on how to run it.

After the chopper left, we proceeded down the hill towards the creek. Maybe it was my imagination, but it appeared to me that First Sergeant Cruz was looking disapprovingly at me as we moved forward, and I had no idea why that would have been the case. I shot him an unkind glance and continued moving towards the creek. When we got to Trooper Kmit, he was still laying where he fell. We had to subject him to one more indignity. Fearing the possibility that his body was booby trapped, we tied a long rope around his ankle, backed away behind cover and then pulled him several feet towards us. He had not been booby trapped but his weapon and web gear were missing. Everyone felt better about reclaiming the body of our brother and we elected to carry him with us in a body bag until we found a reasonably safe LZ to have him picked up.

Troopers Edmonds and Kmit are both remembered on Panel 33 West; Edmonds on Line 62 and Kmit on Line 65. Friendly death toll on my watch as Angry Skipper 6 now stood at ten. Sergeant Goochie survived his wounds but has never come to any Angry Skipper reunions. Lieutenant Derums never thanked me for sending Bruce Adams back to work for him.

****

The Vietnamese Lunar New Year known as Tet occurs around mid-February every year and on that holiday we were supposed to stop where we were and sit out an alleged twenty-four hour truce, even though Tet a year earlier was when the Viet Cong attacked all major cities in South Vietnam. But with Tet still a day away, Stone Mountain 6 from above in the Charlie Charlie gave me some grid coordinates and then directed us to the scene of a fight where the enemy had ambushed a platoon of "Blues." "Blue" is the official color of the Infantry. It was also the nickname for the platoon of Infantry assigned to the 1st Cav's Aviation Battalion.

The mission of the Blues was, in the event of a downed aircraft, to go in and secure the scene until bodies or survivors were recovered. If the aircraft itself was salvageable, they would also secure it until it was lifted out. What apparently happened in this case was, after all personnel and a downed helicopter were lifted out by a CH 47 Chinook, the Blues were attacked by the enemy while they themselves were being lifted out. Helicopter gunships engaged the enemy and drove them off, but not until there was another UH-1D down and several dead Americans on the ground around it. Lifting this downed chopper out was a non-issue, in this case, because it was totaled. It was lifting off the ground when it was hit by a B-40 rocket which knocked off the tail rotor. This bird was never going to fly again.

But, of course, there were bodies to recover. Aerial recon after the crash said it was highly unlikely we were going to find anyone alive at the crash scene. We were not far from the site of the crash and we got there fairly quickly. Time was of the essence since we would need to recover the Blues and air crew bodies for evacuation to the rear and then find a good, defensible position where we would remain during the Tet cease fire.

We approached the clearing where the crashed bird and bodies were and carefully circled the area, securing it to make sure we wouldn't end up like the Blues. With perimeter security in place, my headquarters group, a handful of Infantrymen and the company medics entered the clearing. As we were advised, nobody in that clearing was alive and the helicopter was in pieces. It had gained enough altitude that when the RPG hit it knocking off the tail rotor, the chopper swung violently in two or three complete circles before crashing into the ground and breaking up. As it rapidly circled, all the passengers were thrown out of the open doors. The chopper caught fire after it crashed and the pilot and copilot were burned beyond recognition. The burning chopper set the grass on fire, which spread beyond the wreckage.

One of the dead Blues was several feet from the wreckage, frozen in death in a perfect crawling position as he tried to escape the falling chopper. His head was erect, his arms were staggered out in front of him as he clawed at the ground pulling himself forward. One of his legs was straight out behind him and the other was bent as if ready to push himself forward. The ground fire had burned his ears and nostrils. But what killed him was the still rotating main rotor blade of the chopper which cleaved him neatly in half. There was about a six inch space between his upper and lower halves as though his hands, grabbing at the earth, had pulled his upper body that distance away from his lower half before he realized he was dead.

While we were in the center of the clearing, a chopper came by low and slow and dropped out a bunch of body bags and a box of rubber gloves. Delta Company medics were given the task of collecting dog tags and putting body parts in the bags. I figured they were the least likely people to puke, as I was about to do.

Finally, things were as cleaned up as possible and we called the circling chopper to land and take everything back to mortuary affairs. My map showed a clearing not too far away and Colonel Wood in the Charlie Charlie confirmed the presence of a well-used trail running near the wood line on one side of the clearing. I figured even with this alleged Tet truce, we might just as well be in ambush posture. After all, during the truce, troops on both sides were supposed to cease movement as well as hostilities for twenty-four hours. If anyone did come down our trail at night, they would be violating the truce.

Nobody came down the trail that night but in the early daylight hours, one of our guys saw a uniformed NVA soldier peeking out from behind a tree. The soldier must have realized he'd been seen and fired a single round in our direction, which hit no one. I told Jon Jones to call for some artillery on the NVA's location. He called in the fire mission and it was denied. I took the handset from the FO, identified myself and said, "We just saw and were fired at by an NVA soldier moving near our location in violation of the truce." The original guy who denied our request must have handed his radio handset to his boss because an artillery captain told me his battery was honoring the truce and there would be no fire mission, followed by, "Out!" Ouch!

Oh well, nothing more happened that day nor that night because I suspected, all local NVA knew not to come down our trail.

On our next resupply, Mountain 6 came in also and presented me with a shiny new lieutenant to replace Doug Magruder as the White Skull Platoon leader. Six advised me that the new Skull 6 had done OJT with Alpha Company and was ready to lead a platoon. Preston Karr was the new lieutenant's name. He was tall, blond headed and had movie star good looks. He appeared to be confident and eager to begin troop leading. I introduced him to Bob Babas and David Spingath and called for the White Skull Platoon sergeant who had been acting as the platoon leader following Doug Magruder's medevac on February 5th. Colonel Wood wished us good luck and boarded his helicopter to leave.

Just as much as I disliked Lieutenant Armstrong when I first met him, that's about how much I liked Lieutenant Karr. He did fit in and again, I felt that I had three best platoon leaders in the battalion.

We wouldn't suffer another man killed again until May but, because of us, the NVA would continue to lose men in twos and threes almost nightly. That doesn't mean we weren't scared to death by one near fatal event or another.

One morning while still operating off LZ Saint Barbara, we were told to sit tight in our overnight ambush location and, in fact, were also told to get out the entrenching tools and dig ourselves deeper into the earth. There was going to be an Arclight delivered "danger close" to us and we would be going into that portion of flattened jungle afterwards to conduct a Bomb Damage Assessment (BDA). Of course, we did as we were told.

With jungle canopy overhead and bombers flying at 30,000 feet, we didn't see anything but we clearly felt the earth shake when the bombs landed. When the shaking was over, we saddled up and headed towards the grid coordinates provided by Colonel Wood. As we approached the rectangle of ruin, it became harder to walk due to the blown down trees, tree limbs and craters in our way. This destruction of jungle became worse the farther into it we walked. From the air, perhaps, it looked flattened to the point it would be easy to walk through, but just the opposite was true.

Then, not only was walking tough, but it was becoming quite dangerous. Everything around us was on fire. Smoke and flames were sky high and, at one point, that's all we could see.

It finally fell on Colonel Wood and Major Bramlett in the Charlie Charlie to give us idiot proof directions such as, "...in 100 yards, turn right." If it were left up to us on the ground to find a way out of this inferno, 2/8th Cav would become short one complete rifle company. Everywhere we turned, all we could see was a wall of smoke and fire. Eventually, one of those "turn right's" or "turn left's" actually allowed us to see a corridor to our front which let us walk out of danger.

As far as the BDA, I believe I could accurately report that everything in that half-mile-by-two-mile rectangle was destroyed. As for specifics on what exactly was destroyed besides trees, I haven't a clue. After almost getting roasted, we were told to shoot an azimuth towards LZ Saint Barbara. It was our turn to come onto the LZ for showers, laundry and a brief rest.

We headed towards Saint Barbara knowing that somewhere within easy walking distance of the firebase, we'd have to spend one more night in the bushes before enjoying the showers and other amenities of the LZ. And, of course, we all knew we'd be leaving Saint Barbara, either on foot or by chopper later the same day. The reason for this was, as stated previously, the base belonged to the 25th Infantry Division and Corps artillery. There was simply no room at the inn for another rifle company.

For this night, we picked a trail that really didn't show signs of recent heavy usage by the NVA; but it was a trail and it was a reasonable humping distance from the firebase the next morning. So, signs of recent usage or not, we would still have a platoon on a kill zone with Claymores out as though we expected company. We had no company that night and saddled up for the march to Saint Barbara. I advised the TOC of our estimated arrival at the LZ.

Once on the firebase, it was permissible to breathe a little easier, although the possibility of catching an RPG right in the snot locker always existed. I met with Colonel Wood and Major Bramlett in the TOC. The colonel advised that there had been a complaint about our request for an artillery fire mission, but they were not concerned about it. Neither was I. My thoughts were, if I hadn't gotten in trouble for leaving an S & P trailer full of ammunition in the open back at Quang Tri, I probably wasn't going to get in trouble for the Tet thing. Then Colonel Wood told me that the battalion was going to open and occupy a new firebase closer to Cambodia than we had ever been. After Delta Company would leave Saint Barbara, the next time we were on a firebase would be on LZ Carolyn. (Many years later I would meet Mrs. Wood, Carolyn, and she is indeed a charming lady. I never asked her how she felt about having an LZ named after her but I'm sure she didn't mind.)

I asked the colonel if we would be leaving on foot or by chopper. He told me it would be by chopper. All the 2/8 Cav companies were going to be relocated to the vicinity of the new LZ Carolyn. It would be built using some old materiel salvaged from a former Special Forces camp nearby, and some new materiel flown in, so tight security would be in order around the new LZ while the division engineers brought in the necessary machines, supplies and tools to create the new firebase. I suspected the new LZ would really piss off the NVA as it will sit astride and conduct interdiction operations on their many routes south towards Saigon.

We had a couple of hours to kill before the slicks that would carry us to the vicinity of our new home would arrive, so after my shower and change of uniform I walked around our temporary slice of Saint Barbara talking to my men. Then, unexpectedly, I learned I had just lost my FO, Lieutenant Jon Jones. He was accidently burned by a "friendly" white phosphorous grenade here on Saint Barbara. At the time, I was visiting with my soldiers and by the time I learned about this accident, Jonsey had already been airlifted to a hospital. I felt awful that I hadn't been able to say goodbye to him, nor did I know how badly he was hurt. This happened in early 1969 and I wouldn't see Jonsey again until an Angry Skipper reunion in Las Vegas in 1999. When I did, he still had rosy red cheeks, blond curly hair, bright white teeth and a big smile on his face. His worst burns were apparently elsewhere on his body. I introduced Jonsey to my wife Janine. "Your husband used to call me his fat fucking FO," said Jon with his sparkling smile. Janine and I adopted Jon for the rest of our time in Vegas. I am happy to say I have seen Jon many times now at reunions and I plan to see him at our annual Kentucky Kampout reunion in years to come.

(I made reference earlier in this chapter to talking with "my men." I did that for a reason. Over the years since my Vietnam experiences, I have had occasional PTSD induced nightmares, probably accelerated by some Scotch [thanks General S]. These episodes sometimes scared the hell out of my wife. My first clue that I even had an episode would be when I awoke alone in bed and found Janine sleeping on the couch downstairs. She told me that in yelling and barking commands, the term "My men!" was something I said a lot. After finally joining a VA sponsored Vietnam Veterans Group for about three years, the nightmares have tapered off. However, now that I am writing a book about those experiences, maybe they'll revisit me.)

One thing I picked up after our ordeal by the creek where troopers Kmit and Edmonds died, the men, my men, were referring to the incident as "Colavita Creek." In a way, I was taking that as a compliment because when I first took over the company, I heard frequent reference to a "Grannemann's Hill."

The way I understood it, there was a good sized fight on a hill in their old AO up north and the actions of the Angry Skipper 6 at that time, Rod Grannemann, saved some lives. I believed naming that hill after their CO was a compliment. And I thought the same about "Colavita Creek."

In the long run, though, it apparently didn't matter. After a while I heard no more talk about "Colavita Creek" and realized I hadn't heard any reference to "Grannemann's Hill" in a long time either. So those names really didn't mean much. They were both incidents the troops would rather forget. I just hoped there wasn't a "Colavita Cave" or "Colavita Cliff" in our future.

With showers and clean clothes out of the way, we prepared to be airlifted from the airstrip right in front of Saint Barbara and deposited in what will be our new AO around LZ Carolyn. The insertion of one or two and ultimately four new rifle companies closer to Cambodia would certainly be of interest to the NVA. And when they see bull dozers and road graders being air lifted in, then we will really have their attention.

Since the airstrip in front of Saint Barbara was long enough to accommodate enough choppers to lift the whole company at once, we selected a clearing on the map near our new home which could also accept that number of choppers, although not necessarily in a straight line formation. The company liked it better, and the chopper pilots liked it better, when it was possible to pick us all up and deliver us all in one fell swoop. As close as we were to Cambodia, ambushing should be a very lucrative business, although we were not the closest firebase in the 1st Cavalry Division's entire AO.

We landed a couple of kilometers west of the soon-to-be-built LZ Carolyn, which was about ten or so kilometers due north of LZ Saint Barbara. We were, however, moving into a space that hadn't seen any major American presence before. The small Special Forces Camp that used to be located near where LZ Carolyn was to be built was just that—a small Special Forces camp, similar to the one where the SF captain threw me off the crapper oh so many years ago.

Construction of LZ Carolyn would not be dragged out. The enemy wouldn't let us drag it out. So, soon the air would be buzzing with helicopters of all shapes and sizes bringing in heavy equipment of all shapes and sizes. We operated off LZ Saint Barbara for two months with no home base to defend. Despite the fact that two of my ten dead soldiers were killed on an LZ, the soldiers really felt that life on a firebase is a little safer.

Before leaving Saint Barbara, Colonel Wood and I discussed where Delta Company should begin our ambushing adventures in this new AO, so I shared this information with my platoon leaders and, once we hit the ground, we moved out in our traditional three platoons abreast.

Our first night in ambush in our new AO, we killed three NVA. Perhaps they were going on R & R because they had only their personal weapon and papers with them and they were heading towards Cambodia, not Saigon. We were well into the month of April and hadn't lost any one killed or seriously wounded since "Colavita Creek."

I assumed while the engineers and their equipment worked on the LZ that the battalion would operate as we did while rebuilding LZ Rita, with one company doing perimeter defense, one company out and about but closer in, and two companies out farther searching and destroying. This new AO was proving lucrative as Delta Company continued to kill NVA almost nightly. Like the first few, most of these guys were not carrying heavy loads indicating they were on their way back into Cambodia to pick up more stuff and move it south.

The month of April was slipping away and finally D Company was called in to defend the LZ perimeter. The guys were glad to be going on a firebase again.

Engineer bulldozers had pushed down and cleared away trees in all directions around the firebase. The enemy would have to cross considerable open space to get to the wire. The new bunkers had been dug deeply into the ground and had substantial overhead cover of steel planking and sandbags. They were staggered on the perimeter and built with the 45 degree gun ports in order to cover bunkers on their left and right. They were less susceptible to being taken out by a single B-40 rocket to the front. The TOC was strongly built with thick walls and overhead cover. No one before 2/8 Cav had slept in these newly constructed bunkers nor crapped in our newly built latrines.

After so long in the field with no bunkers or latrines, the guys were happy to have a home again. I thought to myself, *Enjoy it guys, because soon enough we will be back in the bushes searching and destroying and trying to stay alive.*

Eleven

LZ Carolyn

THE MONTH OF APRIL WAS SLIPPING AWAY and I now had over six months in command. No replacement was in sight and I was developing a big problem. I had grown to love the guys of Delta Company. These men, my men, had performed magnificently and I didn't want to be responsible for any deaths or serious injury to any more of them. On the other hand, I didn't want to turn them over to someone else who might be reckless. Someone who would worry more about his career and medals than the lives of these soldiers. Someone who, out of recklessness or stupidity, would get a bunch of them killed. Then I had to stop and think for a second: *Ten guys, so far, have died on my watch. Isn't that a bunch?*

After saying my own personal prayer to God every morning to keep me alive another day, I started adding an additional prayer: "Please, God, don't let there be any contact with the enemy today, except for our nighttime ambush."

Earlier, as I was approaching my sixth month in command, I mentioned to my confidant, artillery FO Jon Jones, that I was going to talk with Mountain 6 about pulling me out as soon as I hit the six month mark. I don't know about other companies in 2/8, but I felt that Delta Company had more than our share of bloody noses. I was worried about getting too cautious and over thinking my actions and causing more guys to die. Jon didn't think that was going to be a move in the best interests of my future in the Army. I sincerely told him I appreciated his advice but later, after Jon had been injured and medevaced, I disregarded his advice and did send a note back to Stone Mountain 6 by a returning resupply bird stating that I thought it was time for me to come out and give some other Infantry captain a chance to command. Every one of us knew that in this environment an unexpected bullet or explosion could be the end of us, and we all lived with that; but I also had what is rightly called the "weight of command" on me since mid-October, and it was getting heavier.

Except in unusual circumstances, the captain is the highest ranking Army officer on the ground and in the fight with his men. I thought of the many times after a fight where guys were wounded or killed, and I had to issue the order to saddle up and move out. I wouldn't have blamed them in the least if they had said, "Hell no!"

A couple of days later, Mountain 6 and 3 flew in to see me and it was to discuss my note. My chat with Colonel Wood and Major Bramlett was pleasant enough. They understood where I was coming from but, to my surprise, the colonel told me there wasn't another captain in the replacement pipeline coming to 2/8. That really surprised me. I imagined there would be Infantry captains stacked up waiting for a chance to command a company in combat. Colonel Wood then offered to send Lieutenant Magruder, now a first lieutenant, out as my replacement if I felt that strongly about coming out. I didn't want that to happen. Doug had already picked up two Purple Hearts and I believed he had done more than his fair share of the fighting. I declined the colonel's kind offer to have Doug replace me and I told him that I would soldier on until a new captain showed up. We shook hands and Stone Mountain 6 and 3 departed leaving me with around one hundred and twenty men I loved like brothers.

Looking at the bright side, after that bloody day, February 5, 1969 ("Colavita Creek"), we had suffered no Delta Company fatalities. We got through the entire month of March and were almost finished with April. We did have some wounded along the way but none life threatening and surely a suitable replacement for me would show up in the month of May, or so I thought. An Infantry captain completing seven months in command of a rifle company was most certainly not a common occurrence in this war. For my part, I vowed to do everything in my power to see that nobody else in my company would die, and continued saying my extra little prayer, "Please God, no enemy contact today (except, you know, the nightly ambush)."

****

Our new AO surrounding LZ Carolyn offered many opportunities for lucrative ambushing. There were many huge open spaces in the jungle, some larger than several football fields laid out side-by-side. Many of them had well-worn trails along one wood line or the other, or both. These open spaces allowed whole companies to be picked up in one lift and moved to another area where they could be landed together at the same time. This was much less risky than doing combat assaults into, or extractions out of, an LZ that required multiple lifts to get a company in and out. Although a major plus for us, there was also a downside. If we were walking from point A to point B and one or more of these gigantic clearings were between these points, the smart thing to do was to walk around them, certainly never to walk through them. This added a lot of distance to the trip. These clearings were large enough that one Infantry company could not adequately secure them for a helicopter lift in or out, so combat assaults into such a clearing required a substantial artillery preparation before an insertion, and extractions required armed helicopters overhead to engage any enemy that wanted to catch us on our way out.

On the last day of April, we had received our resupply on the edge of a large clearing. Running along our side of the clearing was a well-worn trail showing a lot of recent usage. After the resupply bird took off, we put machine gun teams facing up and down the trail and then we moved out of the clearing but not away from it. I put Range Platoon in the wood line parallel to the trail in ambush formation while Cat and Skull wrapped around behind the ambush in our classic "Delta 'bush" formation. It was a lovely day weather-wise and we were in no hurry to be somewhere else at a certain time.

I decided that, on this rare occasion, I would let the troops eat a leisurely C-Rat meal and read their mail from home. When this break was over we would load up our gear and prepare to move out, and that's how it would appear to anyone who might be watching us. We made a pile of our empty C-Ration cans and other garbage in the open between the trail and the wood line. While we were making our trash visible, other troops were setting out Claymores just inside the wood line facing the trail. The Claymores were then covered with grass and other vegetation. With blasting caps inserted, the wires were pulled behind the Claymores back into the bush and marked with a rock or twig so they could be easily located. We then noisily saddled up and moved into the jungle so, if there were any eyes on us, they would lose sight of us. Then, employing all the stealth over a hundred guys could employ, we back-tracked towards the trail and got into our D formation and waited for some customers. We connected the Claymore clappers to the previously deployed wires, and we waited.

After a while, a curious fellow approached our trash pile. He checked out the C ration cans using his finger to scoop out whatever remained inside. Those of us who could see him were amused. This guy was dressed like the Viet Cong I was familiar with from my first tour, in black PJs, Ho Chi Minh sandals and conical straw hat. He could be taken for a local farmer but he had a couple of things going against him. First, the government of South Vietnam had assured the 1st Cavalry Division that there were no friendly civilians in our AO, and second, this guy was carrying the ubiquitous Avtomat Kalashnikov rifle, the AK-47.

After fooling around with our trash for a while, he spotted one of our little piles of grass covering a Claymore. He walked over, brushed away the camouflage and looked at it. Then he picked up the mine and pulled out the wire and blasting cap. Obviously without a clue about what he had in his hands, he put the mine under his arm and walked to the next pile of grass. We were not about to let this guy pick up our Claymores so I gave the soldier in charge of the second Claymore clapper a thumbs down sign. As the man picked up the second Claymore, my man set it off. When this Claymore exploded, the one under the man's arm also exploded turning him into trail mix. Taking him as a prisoner was a chance I was not willing to take with any of my soldiers' lives. He was still in the clearing where our resupply bird had landed and we were deeper into the woods, so I wasn't sending anybody out to grab him. If we made ourselves visible and motioned for him to join us, he could have just as easily fired at us. And, maybe he had friends in the area. The best thing to do with him was what we did. We could have simply shot him and saved two Claymores, but in Vietnam, explosions are often heard regularly all over and do not spark much alarm. U. S. fire bases routinely and randomly fire Harassing and Interdicting (H & I) rounds into the bush. Close-by rifle shots are alarming. Besides, this incident with the little man with the pointy hat gave the guys a good laugh. Good laughs are hard to come by in Vietnam.

****

We finished out the month of April and moved into May. In two more weeks I would have been in command for seven months—and still no word on a replacement.

The number of enemy kills in ambush, not only by Delta Company but by all four of 2/8's rifle companies, must really be pissing the enemy off, I thought. To accomplish what our Intelligence people were saying was the NVA's primary mission in War Zone C, they needed to move south towards the populated areas around Saigon to disrupt the renewed pacification efforts by the South Vietnamese government with, of course, our support. Our job here was to not let them do their job down south. We were regularly killing them as they tried to move men and supplies south, and when we weren't killing them, we were stumbling into their prepositioned supply cachets and stealing their weapons, ammo and rice.

On May 2nd, however, God must not have heard my prayer about no enemy contact. We had come upon a wide trail with signs of much recent activity but it was too soon in the day to set up an ambush. I had planned to move much farther north before stopping for the night. I called in the grid coordinates of the trail at the point where we located it so it could be targeted for some

H & I fire, but our immediate task was to safely cross this trail and move on. As usual in these circumstances, we put two machine gun teams out on the trail covering our flanks. No sooner were the gun teams out than a B-40 rocket slammed into one of the teams killing PFC Neil Shipp Brown and seriously wounding the other member of the gun team. It was a single, apparently well aimed rocket scoring a direct hit on its target. There were no following shots.

We quickly circled the wagons waiting for contact but none came. Most of the guys believed, and still do to this day, that we were being stalked by one or two NVA who found an opportunity, and took it, to kill an American soldier or two. There was still plenty of daylight left to get a medevac in and also to get an aerial recon of our location to see if they could spot anyone tracking us. I called Mountain 6 and apprised him of our situation and requested the medevac and recon. I identified what looked like a suitable LZ not far from our current location and advised the colonel we would be carrying our dead and wounded brothers to this location.

We had gone all the way from February 5th to May 1st without getting anyone killed, but our lucky streak ended on that May 2nd.

Neil Shipp Brown was a Mormon from Salt lake City, Utah. He was college educated and very bright. Soldiers kept tabs, as best they could, on potential job openings both on the LZ or, better yet, in the rear area with the company XO. PFC Brown was the odds on favorite to get the next available job out of the field, probably as a company clerk. Now he was going to the rear, not as a company clerk, but in a body bag. Neil Shipp Brown is remembered on Panel 26 West, Line 97 on the Vietnam Wall.

Generally speaking, after a contact like we'd just had, chances of killing anyone in an ambush that night in the same general area are not good. Chances of getting swarmed by a much larger enemy force are much better. We moved away from the medevac LZ and looked for a good spot to dig in and be prepared to defend ourselves. We plotted DTs and hunkered down for the night. While in this defensible posture, Colonel Wood and I spoke by radio and agreed that our presence in this neighborhood was compromised and we would be lifted out the next day and moved elsewhere in the AO.

The 1st Cavalry Division soldiers had gotten quite good at performing false insertions and extractions. These maneuvers were designed to confuse the enemy. A false insertion goes like this: A flight of choppers comes into an LZ previously prepped by artillery. Troops can be easily seen sitting in the open doors of these birds and even standing on the skids. We want them visible. Between the troops blocking the doors or standing on the skids, there are no other soldiers on board. The choppers touch down and instead of unloading the troops, they duck back into the choppers and lie flat on the floor as the choppers lift off. This maneuver is designed to make the NVA believe a bunch of U.S. soldiers has just landed in their backyard. The false extraction works in reverse. Empty appearing choppers touch down on an LZ. Then, on takeoff, troops who have been lying on the floor now sit up and become visible as the choppers lift off, hopefully causing the NVA to believe we just pulled a bunch of soldiers out.

Neither Colonel Wood nor I believed a false extraction would work in this case since the enemy that killed Trooper Brown were obviously very close to us when they took their shot, and they were probably still keeping an eye on us. We decided better to circle the wagons, dig some deep holes, plot our artillery DTs and wait until tomorrow when we would be flown several kilometers away and be able go back to searching and destroying in a new neighborhood. In a few days, it would again be time for Delta Company to return to LZ Carolyn and pull perimeter security. But we still had a few days and nights left in the field to hopefully repay the enemy for killing Trooper Neil Brown. On the evening of May 3rd, we were again preparing, hopefully, for a night of Claymores and gook killing. We had no way of knowing that our enemy in this AO, the NVA 95-C regiment, had pulled back to a safe training area to rehearse for an all-out assault on LZ Carolyn. Because of that, no one walked into our ambush that night. In addition to no kills the prior night, nothing happened all day or all night on May 4th.

On the evening of May 5th, we found a gorgeous trail running along the southern wood line of one of those massive clearings. There were plenty of fresh foot and bicycle prints, although most of the prints appeared to be moving towards Cambodia. Frankly, we didn't care which way they were moving when we killed them. We were definitely stopping for the night in this location. Not only did this trail look like a happy hunting ground, but we didn't have enough time before nightfall to move around this massive clearing in the direction we were going. So, we were stopping a bit earlier than usual with some significant daylight left. We plotted our DTs for the night and guys dug some shallow fighting positions and started opening C-Rats.

Then I was notified by my platoon on the ambush that there was some significant movement to our left front. I went forward to have a look. I wished we'd had a set of binoculars with us but we did not really need them that much in the jungle. In the distance, even without binoculars, I could still see many men crossing a break in the surrounding trees. They were heading in the direction of LZ Carolyn. I called Colonel Wood and advised him, "The NVA in force are heading for LZ Carolyn tonight. We are watching a never ending line of gooks crossing a clearing across from our location." I gave him the coordinates of the crossing point and assured him we would be out of harm's way of any artillery fire the LZ wanted to place on that location. "In fact," I said, "my artillery FO can direct the fire from here."

Shortly after our conversation, artillery fire began landing in and around the crossing point. My FO gave the Fire Direction Center some tweaking of the incoming rounds and we knew the enemy was being punished. But, as the fire let up, they kept coming. I was hoping that these bad guys believed they were victims of random H & I fire rather than it being actually observed fire by eyes on the ground. Eventually, the movement across the clearing stopped, meaning that they redirected their movement away from that spot, or everyone who needed to cross the clearing had done so.

Soon darkness descended and we could no longer see the crossing point. I called my platoon leaders to the CP and told them, if they didn't already know, "Carolyn is going to be hit hard tonight. Our position is known by battalion, brigade and division headquarters so we shouldn't have to worry about any incoming friendly fire from Spooky or the Cobra gunships. Still, we have to be prepared to light our position up in the case of any spill-over friendly fire or attack by the NVA, so keep your strobe lights handy. In the morning, we need to be watchful for NVA stragglers trying to make their way back home."

The fight started just before midnight with the usual mortars and rockets followed by small arms fire going in both directions. Soon the sky over Carolyn was lit up and from four kilometers away we could see a glow in the sky. Soon we heard the belch of Spooky and the swoosh and explosion of rockets fired by the Cobras. We would hear those sounds all night until either the early morning light sent the NVA packing, or until they raised their colors over LZ Carolyn. If that should be the outcome, Delta Company would be in a very difficult situation.

Having given the LZ some warning, I felt it was highly unlikely that the NVA would take the firebase. My plan, when we started moving later in the day, was to move towards Carolyn. I figured Charlie Company, no doubt, would take casualties and might even be understrength to the point they couldn't adequately hold the perimeter. Captain Gonzales had finished his tour in Vietnam a while back and Charlie Company was now commanded by my friend, Captain Skip Taylor. (Years later when he would talk about the fight to defend LZ Carolyn, I used to jerk his chain by saying, "What was the big deal, we told you they were coming?" I believe Skip knows I am only kidding as he and Charlie Company fought like hell all night to save Carolyn.)

When we finally got back to Carolyn, we would discover just how close the gooks came to taking the base. It was obvious from radio transmissions that the NVA had breached the wire in some places. The large explosion we heard that also lit up the sky, we would learn, was the intentional ignition of aviation fuel drums by the defenders, which created a wall of fire effectively ending the NVA push onto the LZ from the south. We also learned later how critical was the part played by the artillery in defending the base and keeping the 95-C Regiment out. Specifically, their use of 105mm Howitzers firing Bee Hive rounds directly into the attackers, which would leave some gook corpses still nailed to trees when we returned to Carolyn.

But before we started packing to move to Carolyn, we decided to stay put and wait for the stragglers. As usual, the NVA broke off the attack at daybreak. Later in the morning of May 6th, we did have visitors. Some dazed looking NVA retreating from Carolyn ran into, not our ambush, but the two platoons to the rear of the ambush. There were several of them traveling in a group, not as individuals. Most still carried a weapon, which was cause for us to kill them. All were ragged and filthy and appeared dazed. My guys said they reminded them of movie zombies. Then, in a real shocker, one of the dazed and dirty communists actually walked into our perimeter. Once he was inside the formation, everyone was ready to shoot him but held off for fear of hitting a brother soldier. This gook had no weapon and continued to move forward rapidly and before we knew it, he had walked out through the ambush platoon into the open field. He moved several yards away from us then dropped down on his back, waving his arms and screaming. While trying to decide what to do about him, a Loach appeared overhead and lit up this whacked out gook with a mini gun. Then, on the battalion net, the Loach pilot said, "Skipper 6, don't forget to add that guy to your body count," as he turned his little bird back in the direction of Carolyn.

Before moving out, I checked with Mountain 6 to advise him we were moving towards the LZ if he needed us. Six replied that Alpha Company was closing in on Carolyn to relieve Charlie Company as we spoke and he gave me a set of grid coordinates to move to and continue with search-and-destroy and ambush operations.

On May 10th, we did return to LZ Carolyn and relieved Alpha Company on the perimeter. On the night of May 12th, an enemy B-40 rocket scored a direct hit on one of our bunkers killing another Delta trooper, my 12th dead Delta trooper. His name was George Arthur Brown from Whaleyville, Virginia. Just as a single explosion on a bunker had killed Raymond Joseph Ahern on LZ Rita on November 26, 1968, and another had killed trooper Elliott Velez-Rodriguez also on Rita on January 21, 1969, so did George Arthur Brown become KIA by a rocket on an LZ, but this time, Carolyn (George is remembered on Panel 25 West, Line 62).

But this explosion was not a mystery like the one that killed Eliot Velez-Rodriguez. This explosion followed a sharp hissing sound made by a B-40 rocket when it leaves the launcher. We directed counter battery fire in the direction from which we believed the rocket came. I reported the death by radio to Colonel Wood and he directed me to come to the TOC.

When I entered, he demanded to know why trooper George Brown wasn't inside his bunker. I was stunned by the question. You can order your men to stay inside the bunkers but then you better plan on having a roving bunker patrol to ensure they are following the order. Many of these grunts who spend three-quarters of their time in the field with no cover available just don't want to sleep inside the bunkers. Maybe they're claustrophobic. Maybe the rats moved in again.

Although the newly designed and reinforced bunkers staggered along the LZ perimeter with forty-five degree firing ports proved their worth to Charlie Company during the fight with the 95-C Regiment, most of my troops did not like them because they couldn't see directly to their front. Maybe George was the one to be on duty and he was outside the bunker so he could see to his front as well as to the left and right. Anyway, my conversation with the colonel was brief and it never came up again.

Within the last ten days, I had lost another two of my men. *Where the hell was my replacement?* My friendly body count was now twelve. (During our annual reunion in Tennessee in 2014, Bob Babas and I were discussing LZ Carolyn. Bob told me he only suffered one KIA during his tenure as Range 6. This casualty was George Arthur Brown on LZ Carolyn. He added that it shouldn't have happened because he had ordered his troops to stay in their bunkers overnight.)

****

It turns out that on the night of May 12, 1969, the gooks were not yet through with Carolyn, as they hit it again around midnight. This contact, however, was more of a probe than a serious attack. These gooks were apparently trying to figure out where our machine guns were located so they could be destroyed later in another real attack. I was pleased with the discipline shown by my machine gunners as none of them fired their weapons. Rifles and grenade launchers were sufficient for this probe. This probe was short but costly to the enemy. The engineers had pushed the tree line back so far from the firebase that these guys had to expose themselves as they tried to gather information.

The next morning, more NVA dead littered the ground around Carolyn and there were probably more of them just inside the tree line. The severe damage done to the 95-C Regiment on the 6th had not yet been entirely cleaned up with a number of the rotting dead from that fight still lying around, although it wasn't hard to tell the ones just killed from those a week old. A good sized bulldozer had just been flown into the LZ with the assigned task of plowing a large trench between the tree line and the LZ perimeter. The operator then had the gruesome duty of plowing the dead into the trench. A platoon would be providing security for the dozer and driver. This action was absolutely necessary to alleviate the stench which was literally sickening. If we were to stay on Carolyn, this mess had to be made to go away.

The next morning I went out with a group of my guys to collect weapons and papers from the recently killed. Another patrol went inside the tree line surrounding the LZ to look for more bodies, weapons and papers. I was hoping that George Arthur Brown was my last one KIA. *Twelve is certainly a bunch!*

While still outside the wire, I got a call from Cat 6 leading the patrol inside the wood line. He advised me that Corporal James Robert Dunkle, newly assigned to the company, was looking into a thicket at an enemy soldier he believed was dead. That enemy was soon to die but not before he shot Corporal Dunkle dead.

Trooper Dunkle was so new most of the company had not met him. (When the D 2/8 Honor Roll was pieced together years later at one of the first Angry Skipper reunions, Corporal Dunkle was not on the list. It would be a few more years before one of the guys on patrol with him when he was killed pointed out our omission and we put James Robert Dunkle on the Honor Roll. He is also remembered on Panel 25 West, Line 98 of the Wall.)

Then, from out of nowhere, my replacement arrived. Captain Ed Livingston, an OCS graduate and former Special Forces soldier. I didn't have the words to describe how glad I was to be stepping out of command.

Unlike my meeting with Buddy Garner on LZ Joe so long ago, I was going to have time to personally introduce Ed to his officers, NCOs and soldiers. I was going to tell him how we had been operating and ambushing and I would share with him my opinion of his subordinate leaders based on my experience working with them. Before Ed left the LZ with his company, I had formed my opinion of him and it was a good one. I liked Ed then and I love him like a brother today. (Ed and I have been at reunions together where it was clear that the men who worked for us appeared to genuinely like us both. That's the best a company commander in combat can ask for.)

As for me, I was going right back to work as the battalion S-2. The battalion had an excellent S-2 named Dave Milton who joined Stone Mountain about the same time I became Skipper 6. He was so good that he was asked for by name by the division G-2, and that's where he went. I was happy to stay with the Stone Mountain boys for my remaining two months in country. But before anything else happened, Karl Derums, who tracked everyone's eligibility for an out of country R & R, reminded me that I was overdue for one. I almost declined to take it but everyone insisted I should go, and I'm glad they did.

With ten months in country, I knew my seniority could bump people with lesser time, regardless of their rank, to get to where I wanted to go, which was Australia. The last time I heard, Australia was a land with round eyed women who spoke a language I thought I could understand, maybe. But strange things do happen.

Troops going on R & R process through the same depots as the soldiers arriving and departing Vietnam. At the depot in Long Binh, I ran into my old roommate from the Advance Course, Major Ed Yago, AKA, Pies Max. In short order, he had convinced me to go with him to Hong Kong.

Hong Kong was known for its tailor shops where guys could have custom made suits, sports coats, slacks and stuff made for a fraction of the cost back in the States. I was never known as a clothes horse but I decided to get a couple of things made in Hong Kong. I was sure Ed and I were going to enjoy the place. The tailor shops were also known for their all-you-can drink policy while you look through men's fashion magazines to decide what you want made. I am officially blaming it on that drinking policy and, in particular, Chivas Regal, because everything I ordered was out of date as soon as the tailor cut the cloth. I ordered narrow lapels on my suit and sports jackets when, back in the World, everyone was wearing wide lapels. I ordered flat front slacks when pleats were in. I would, however, keep those clothes until they came back in style and I was determined to keep my weight down so I could wear them. Ed and I both drank too much after ten months with only a couple of beers a couple of times. We saw the sights, ate like pigs and hit a couple of night spots for tourists and then, poof, it was time to go back to Vietnam and the war.

On the flight back I began planning how I would perform the duties of Stone Mountain 2. I was comfortable with Colonel

Wood and sure my last two months would fly by. When I got back to the battalion, Lieutenant Derums told me the battalion had abandoned LZ Carolyn and moved to another LZ closer to Cambodia named LZ Becky. And I wasn't going to be Stone Mountain 2. Karl handed me orders directing me to report to Division Headquarters and become part of the G-3 shop.

Then Karl dropped a bomb on me. While working off LZ Becky, three Delta Company troopers had been KIA. They were Wayne Eric Garven of Mount Vernon, Ohio; Richard Neal White of Golden Valley, New Mexico; and Lieutenant John Preston Karr of Kenner, Louisiana. All three were killed in an action that took place on May 25th, nine days after I relinquished command of Delta Company. Private Garvin, Lieutenant Karr and Corporal White are honored on Panel 24W, lines 102, 104 and 109 respectively.

Maybe I would have been killed if I were still Skipper 6. Maybe ten guys would have been killed instead of three. I wasn't foolish enough to believe that if I were still Skipper 6 those guys would still be alive. I took my newly printed orders from Karl and set out to find a flight to division.

Twelve

Captain Ambush

MEETING LIEUTENANT COLONEL JACK GIBNEY for the second time was pretty much like meeting him for the first time. He was seated at his desk looking over papers and only glanced up at me and then looked back down. No, "Nice to see you again." No, "You did a hell of a job as Skipper 6." Nothing in the way of a friendly greeting, which was disappointing because I felt like I had paid my dues with the 1st Cavalry Division. While still not looking at me, he gave me a verbal rough draft of my new job.

"You will be working for me in G-3, training," he said. "I want you to develop an outline for an ambush seminar which you will take with you to each 1st Cav LZ. You will be the moderator of this seminar for each rifle company of the nine battalions. We're going to use you and your seminar to spread knowledge and experience around about killing the most enemy and taking the fewest casualties through the use of effective ambush techniques. Your immediate supervisor is Major Art Kinzel, Chief of Training. Any questions, Captain?"

"No, sir," I replied.

The G-3 shop had two main responsibilities, the first being Operations, which involved everything to do with the maneuver elements of the division, except training, and the other responsibility being Training. Without ever having thought about where my Delta Company might rank on the top ten list for killing NVA in ambush, there was no doubt in my mind we were high on that list, maybe even on the very top.

This seminar assignment told me that D 2/8 had been recognized at division level as being very good bunch of gook killers by ambush. It never occurred to me to keep a running total of the numbers of enemy we killed, specifically, in ambush. I always reported my numbers to battalion and I knew these numbers were being recorded in duty logs, certainly at battalion, and probably at brigade and division. There could be no other reason why I was picked to do this seminar. Then it hit me that my use of full company-sized ambushes, which I had known all along was not in conformity with U. S. Army Infantry School doctrine, could be exposed. That landed on me like a ton of bricks. I never told Colonel Henry nor Colonel Wood how we were ambushing nor did I say anything to the other company commanders. Then I had some passing thoughts about what the punishment would be for ignoring Fort Benning and Infantry School tactical doctrine. But then it occurred to me that possibly the word was out. Maybe everyone knew how Delta did ambushes and they were all okay with it. I remember telling my guys that if we kill lots of bad guys and collect lots of their weapons, maps and documents, no one will care how we're doing our ambushes.

We did kill lots of gooks while minimizing the risk to ourselves. How could anyone *not* be okay with that?

All this stuff was going through my head as I moved my belongings into a room I would share with another captain. Turns out my roommate, Captain Tom Hartman, and I went through the same IOBC and Ranger schools together, although we didn't really know each other. I didn't even know what his job was at division but, at the present time, I was worried about my own job. As far as roommates go, with only two months remaining on the tour, I could live with Dracula, provided he kept his fangs to himself, so rooming with Captain Hartman was fine with me.

I started out really stressed, wondering if there was any penalty to pay for not doing things the way the Infantry School taught. I told myself, "If there was, I'm sure it won't affect my DEROS. After all, the final product of our efforts is what counts and Delta Company delivered the goods." Now I'm stressing less.

As Colonel Gibney said when he told me what I'd be doing, the purpose of these seminars was to "share knowledge and experience" about ambushing. I wasn't actually going to be teaching Ambushing 101. During these seminars I could pluck information from other officers and NCOs of the battalions about how they did ambushes and share it with other companies. I might even toss out the concept of company-size ambushes, without even mentioning that's what we did, and check the reaction. The more information I got from the first few seminars, the more ideas I could share with the next bunch of guys.

Soon I felt much better, calm even. I just went through the usual nut-roll I go through when I overthink a problem. Still, I had a hard time sleeping that first night at division even though I was probably the safest I'd been since arriving in-country ten months earlier. There were deep layers of perimeter fencing around headquarters, countless tons of sandbags and steel planking on buildings, multiple guard posts manned 24/7 and the wood line had been pushed way back from the compound so that the enemy would have to cross an unacceptable amount of cleared space to even reach the wire. Additionally, instant gunship support was available due to the co-location of the Division Aviation Battalion.

The compound itself must have been a school of some kind because my room was in a wing with a row of similar rooms—like a college dorm. Whatever the building had been, it was now hardened with tons of sandbags piled on the roof tops.

Also, my roommate had gone to great additional lengths to protect himself from the occasional rocket or mortar round. I don't know how he did it, but he had hauled in a number of large, curved, corrugated steel culvert sections and arranged them over the entire length of his bunk, which he would now have to slide in and out of like a sleeping bag. On top of the culvert, filled sandbags were arranged to completely cover it. All this would probably protect him in the event of a direct mortar or rocket hit on the roof. But, if he had to get out of bed fast, say, due to a breech in the wire by a thousand gooks, or just an urgent need to pee, he would be in deep trouble!

I unloaded my stuff into the empty wooden dresser closest to the bed that hadn't been turned into a bunker, and my thoughts turned back to my ambush project. I decided I would indeed share with my Infantry brothers some of the stuff Delta Company did, like the Claymore keyboard. Another item to share would be our triangle 'bush in the case of a trail intersection where both trails look good for an ambush. Who could argue with the logic of placing a platoon on each trail at the intersection with the third platoon wrapping around behind both 'bushes?

Anyhow, now that I was no longer in panic mode, I set off to meet with Major Kinzel to see what my other duties might be. The major was a stocky, bald man with, it seemed to me, a lot of energy. He advised me that he was aware my principal task was to get the ambush seminar off the ground and he would allow me maximum time to do this. He also wanted to see what I came up with before sharing anything with Colonel Gibney. I was fine with that.

We were now into the final week of May, 1969, and the major told me I would have the remainder of May to hammer out a seminar outline, or lesson plan, and that the division would like to put the show on the road sometime in June. I frequently had to schedule time with Colonel Gibney to show him my progress, and that's where the timeline began to fall on its ass. The colonel was a busy man. He was frequently not on the Headquarters LZ, but out in the Cav AO meeting with battalion commanders, or coordinating 1st Cav operations with adjacent divisions. When I did get on his calendar, he continually made minor changes to my outline, but I think that was more because he could, rather than the changes were needed. I worked for this man twice but never got the feeling I was one of his favorites.

The month of June was coming to a close and the order from Division HQ announcing the seminars had not yet gone out. The result of the delay allowed me to do more for Major Kinzel, so I was busy and the major was happy.

Finally, very close to the beginning of July, I had some quality time with Colonel Gibney and the project was about to be launched. As an introduction, I put together what I thought were some common sense reasons all companies could agree on and which should make them want to ambush rather than sit quietly in the dark, hoping the enemy would pass by and not fuck with them. My mantra was, "Don't be satisfied with half-assed ambushes and allow a whole bunch of gooks you could have killed remain unscathed and have to be engaged again in the future."

Why we want to conduct ambush operations:
   1. At company and platoon level, the surprise ambush is consistently the best method to use to kill the enemy with minimal friendly casualties.
   2. Success at killing the enemy by ambush and high troop morale are directly related.

3. Enemy soldiers who die or are captured in our kill zone will not have to be fought later in bunker complexes.
4. Ambushing the enemy on his trails will hurt his morale and make him have to find new ways to move troops and supplies.
5. Killing enemy logisticians who are trying to preposition supplies for main force units will disrupt their timeline for offensive action and deny them the food, weapons and other supplies they need, which are now in our hands.

On July 4, 1969, the order establishing the Ambush Seminar Program was finally published:

DEPARTMENT OF THE ARMY
HEADQUARTERS, 1ST CAVALRY DIVISION (AIRMOBILE)
AVDAGT4   JULY 1969
SUBJECT: Ambush Tactics and Techniques
TO:

Commanding Officer, 1st Brigade, 1st Cav Div (AM)
Commanding Officer, 2d Brigade, 1st Cav Div (AM)
Commanding Officer, 3d Brigade, 1st Cav Div (AM)
Commanding Officer. 1st Battalion, 5th Cavalry, 1st Cav Div (AM)
Commanding Officer, 2d Battalion, 5th Cavalry, 1sr Cav Div (AM)
Commanding Officer, 1st Battalion, 7th Cavalry, 1st Cav Div (AM)
Commanding Officer, 2d Battalion, 7th Cavalry, 1st Cav Div (AM)
Commanding Officer, 5th Battalion, 7th Cavalry, 1st Cav Div (AM)
Commanding Officer, 1st Battalion, 8th Cavalry, 1st Cav Div (AM)
Commanding Officer, 2d Battalion, 8th Cavalry, 1st Cav Div (AM)
Commanding Officer, 1st Battalion, 12th Cavalry, 1st Cav Div (AM)
Commanding Officer, 2d Battalion, 12th Cavalry, 1st Cav Div (AM)

1. In the eight months that the Division has been operating in III CTZ, the importance of effective ambushing has been proven conclusively. The ambush is our most efficient tactic, since, in comparison with other modes of operation, it produces the most favorable enemy/friendly kill ratio. Although our ambushing has been relatively successful to date and our skill in this tactic appears to be increasing, we still have much room–and much need–for improvement. One step in this direction is the sharing of the wealth of knowledge on this subject which has been accumulated by individual, small unit leaders in all of our battalions. The pooling of this knowledge cannot but pay dividends in terms of increased combat effectiveness throughout the Division.

2. Effective immediately, a program will be implemented to provide a Division-wide exchange of ideas and expertise through the medium of a series of informal seminars for small-unit Infantry leaders. This program will be supervised by ACofS, G3, with seminars conducted at battalion fire bases at a time designated by the battalion commander concerned. An Ass't G3 (and former company commander) will be the moderator for the seminars; his function will be to lead a discussion among the officers and non-commissioned officers of the company occupying the firebase, drawing from them their ideas on ambushing and providing them with lessons learned derived from the experiences of others.

3. The scheduling of these seminars will remain as flexible as possible. It is expected that as a company rotates from the field onto the firebase the battalion commander concerned will request (through operational channels) a specific time for the conduct of the seminar. Requests should contain as much lead time as possible and must reach this Headquarters not later than 1800 hours of the day preceding the date requested.

Battalion commanders are responsible for ensuring the best possible physical arrangement for these seminars. They are also encouraged to submit recommendations for improvement in this program to ACofS, G3.

> FOR THE COMMANDER:
> ROBERT M. SHOEMAKER
> COLONEL, GS
> CHIEF OF STAFF

Obviously, I was the "Ass't G3 (and former company commander)" cited in the order. Just about everyone at Division HQ knew this project was in the works and as folks found out that I was the project officer, I picked up the new nickname of "Captain Ambush."

Prior to my first trip to a firebase, in my last meeting with Colonel Gibney, he put his O.K. on the seminar package, but then threw a monkey wrench into the works. He demanded that I take with me and use a cassette tape recorder. *Now, I'm uncomfortable again. The troops will not be happy to see this recording device. It will put a serious chill on any free and open discussion. Quite frankly, how could the man be that out of touch with his soldiers?*

But, I had my orders.

My first seminar took place on July 12, 1969, on an LZ named Ike. The first participating battalion was the 2d of the 5th Cavalry. The designation of the actual company and the commander of that company will remain nameless. This captain and twelve members of his company attended the seminar. The first question directed at me was, "Why the tape recorder?" I lied and said, "I'm the only one who will be listening to the recording. It's just so I can write up our discussion." And, as our discussion went along, I was the one being educated.

This company's method of ambushing should have been drowned at birth. Like my Delta Company, they also used a full company-sized formation; however, that's where the similarity ended. This company circled the wagons while sitting directly on the targeted trail, overlapping it on both sides. Their only kill zones were where their perimeter crossed the trail at either end. That is why the company commander and name of the company will remain nameless. It is now so many years after the war that no one is going to get in trouble for stupidity in the field back then, and I don't want to embarrass anyone either; but first off, if they manage to kill anyone at all, it's only going to be in one "kill zone" or the other—not both. The enemy is not likely to be moving in both directions at the same time on the same trail. The "kill zone" that gets the action is only going to kill the first one or two guys walking point. In this ridiculous configuration there is no good way to use Claymores for maximum punch. The first one or two gooks walking down the trail are dead meat but the ten, fifteen, maybe twenty or more behind them will all live to fight another day.

I threw out some more sensible ways to ambush but the collective look from the group told me they liked what they were doing. We talked about the frequency of resupply. This company took resupply every three days but they insisted on, and apparently got, a hot meal with their resupply. The three days part was alright but, in my book, the hot meal part was not. The hot meal was delivered in mermite containers and these were not expendable items. This meant that after the hot meal the chopper is going to have to return to pick up the containers and whatever else they brought in which must be returned. The other option was to carry the kitchen crap with them and exchange it on the next resupply for another hot meal and a new set of kitchen crap. The reason given for the hot meal was troop morale. In my opinion, killing a bunch of enemy soldiers and coming out of it without any casualties is the best thing for morale. Next, because noise and light discipline are critical in a night ambush, we discussed punishments to be assessed for violators. Several soldiers wanted serious punishments for these guys. Others felt that trying to assess severe UCMJ punishment only leads to the violators being returned to the rear area, out of the field, where no one ever hears what their punishment was, if anything at all happened to them. Others in the company said they preferred internal sanctions to correct the problem people. I suggested constant pressure by company leaders on the need for noise and light discipline in order to keep each other alive.

I didn't know what the reaction was going to be back at division when they learned this company of over one hundred men was satisfied with killing one or two gooks in ambush.

As the discussion progressed, I noticed eyes were frequently focused on the tape recorder. I had some serious concerns that during our discussion, some unkind remarks might be made about leadership of the battalion, brigade or division and, despite the presence of the recorder, it happened. I believe it was a young NCO who said, "Those fucking pinheads sitting at division in their ivory towers ought to try doing some of this shit themselves." That comment disregarded the fact that those pinheads probably did some of this shit, only in Korea or WW II. I was totally surprised that, even with the recorder running, some unthinking officers and NCOs did utter some unbelievably stupid things, which were not going to be appreciated back at headquarters.

So, after my very first seminar on LZ Ike, I was again flirting with a possible court martial because, rather than let Colonel Gibney or any of the other brass at division hear the pinhead comment and some other insulting remarks, I erased selected portions of the tape.

I met with Colonel Gibney shortly after returning from my first seminar. Before playing the tape, which could cause me to face some sort of punishment, I did tell the colonel that, "The tape recorder did get a lot of negative attention before we even started our discussion." Then I held my breath and pushed the "Play" button. To me, the silent portions of the tape were quite loud. After listening to the doctored tape, the colonel turned to me and said, "Forget about taking the recorder with you." Halle-fucking-lujah! I would live to fight another day.

****

Throughout my participation in this ambush seminar project, which had me flying to all 1st Cavalry LZs, as well as the First Team Academy, officers and NCOs continued to talk openly about using trip flares in the middle of the kill zone, as though that was the only way to ambush. To me, using a trip flare within the kill zone effectively reduces the size of the kill zone by fifty percent or more. In one seminar, a company commander explained that he used two trip flares in the kill zone spaced a few yards apart so that when one of the flares goes off, his people would know which direction the enemy was traveling. My thoughts were, *Who gives a shit which way they were traveling? Check out the dead bodies in the morning and you will have a pretty good idea which way they were traveling!* Every time the subject of trip flares came up, I tried to make an argument against using them but I doubt that changed anyone's mind. I hoped our leaders would notice the trip flare discussions in my after action reports and flat ban the practice of using them (which would probably still not eradicate their use). I could tell in my discussions with units that used trip flares in their ambushes, these devices fit well into their comfort zone. I think they believed, without the noise and unexpected flash of the exploding flare to wake them all up, there might be a number of slit throats as well as friendly deaths by small arms before they could defend themselves.

(At this point in my story, let me state for the record that the U. S. Army Infantry School ambush doctrine did not endorse the use of trip flares in the kill zone of an ambush, at least when I was a young captain it didn't.)

****

My DEROS was August 9, 1969 and it was drawing closer. Although I had been on all of the 1st Cavalry fire bases, I had not reached every rifle company for one reason or another. There were some scheduling hiccups and other legitimate reasons why this hadn't happened. Someone commented that I may have to stay beyond my DEROS to get to the rest of the companies, but it wasn't anyone in charge who offered that thought and I chose to ignore it. I believed that not even the commanding general could interfere with my DEROS without just cause.

In the Army, when one captain's tour of duty is finished, another captain is assigned to take over those duties, and that's the way it works. The DEROS is the actual date the soldier is supposed to be wheels up and out of the combat zone. That meant I had to be released early enough to make my way to the replacement depot.

On July 27th, after doing two different seminars on two different fire bases, I was informed by Major Kinzel that Colonel Gibney had left the division to meet his own DEROS and a new G-3 was in the saddle. The new G-3 was my old battalion commander, Lieutenant Colonel Richard Wood. Although I worked for Colonel Gibney twice during this tour of duty, neither time did I work for him for a full thirty days, so he never wrote an evaluation of my job performance. That was fine with me. And although Colonel Wood and I knew each other, I would not be serving under him for the required thirty days, so my job performance on Division Headquarters staff is memorialized in a fine OER on me written by Major Art Kinzel.

Becoming "Captain Ambush" was a great and totally unexpected way to finish my year with the 1st Cavalry Division. Thinking back to the end of the Advance Course at Fort Benning and the ordeal of trying to decide which unit I wanted to serve with on my second tour in Vietnam, I picked the right one.

Now, before I was to begin hitchhiking my way by air to the freedom bird which would take me back to the World, it was time to begin thinking about where I wanted to be stationed next. That didn't involve much thinking because, as usual, I wanted to go back to Northern Virginia, the Washington, D.C. suburbs, and resume pub crawling and socializing in the 'Hood. I was only 28 years old with no plans yet on becoming a married/family man.

My dad long ago retired from the Army and was now a mortgage banker, whatever that was. Whatever it was, it gave my dad opportunities to meet and befriend a few prominent general officers, both active and retired, which would have never been the case while he was still in the Army.

In a letter, he asked me if I wanted him to ask a four-star acquaintance for help getting assigned near our home in the Washington Metropolitan Area. I replied by letter, "Yes. I do." This without any consideration on my part for what might actually be a career enhancing assignment elsewhere.

When a four-star speaks (or scribbles a note) people pay attention. I would be receiving orders assigning me to the Combat Arms Branch, Combined Arms Division, of the U. S. Army Engineer Center and School at Fort Belvior, Virginia. I was happy to get this news, but at the same time, I was beginning to get concerned about using general officer influence to get me assigned, again, back home. I felt surely, at some point, I was going to try to play this game one time too many and there would be consequences.

But, in the meantime, it was Home Sweet Home.

Thirteen

LZ Home

I COMPLETED A FULL YEAR IN VIETNAM, SEVEN MONTHS as a company commander, and as I look back, I managed to avoid doing some of the dangerous and stupid things I did on my first tour. That is, until just before I left Division Headquarters. That's when I approached an Army doctor, a friend who had been the battalion surgeon for 2/8 and was now also at Division HQ. I told him, "I would like to savor every minute of my flight back to the World." I asked him, "Can you give me something to keep me awake for my entire flight home?"

He responded, "You mean something so you can sleep, don't you?"

I repeated, "No. I want to stay awake during the whole flight. I want to enjoy every second that I get farther away from Vietnam."

He told me to check with him before I left the headquarters compound and he'd have something for me. I did so and he gave me a couple of pills and said, "These will do what you want, but I don't know why you want to do it."

I took these pills the morning of my departure just before I got in line for the plane with my boarding pass clenched tightly in my fist. Again, like the trip over, it was a contract civilian airlines 707 which would be taking us home. And, just like the cabin crew promised a year earlier as we got off the plane, they were here for us, welcoming us on board and, "So happy to be of service to you brave warriors," even though it was a different airline and a different cabin crew.

Whatever those pills were, they did exactly what I wanted but, as I sat in my seat somewhere between Saigon and San Francisco, eyes wide open while everyone else on the plane was fast asleep, I realized I probably had made a bad decision. *What the hell was I thinking?* From San Francisco I flew wide awake to Chicago. Later, as I was killing two hours waiting for a connection at O'Hare, I had a passing fear that I might fall asleep and miss the connection to Dulles International Airport. But there was absolutely no cause for concern. That wasn't going to happen. I couldn't sleep either on the connecting flight from O'Hare to Dulles, nor during the forty-five minute taxi ride from the airport to my parents' home.

Once in the house, I called my father at his office and he came right home. We decided not to call my mother at her job in a local department store but to surprise her instead. When she walked in the door that evening, we yelled. "Surprise!" and unscrewed the cap from a bottle of Mom's Ripple wine. Later, I called and spoke with my brothers, Frank and Billy, and finally crawled into bed and slept for twenty-four hours straight.

Mom told me that friends had stopped by to see me but no one could wake me up. She further allowed that if I hadn't awakened soon, she was going to call rescue. Staying awake was a completely dumb-ass idea. But, it didn't get anyone killed. It was mid-August and I had thirty days leave to use or lose before I reported to Fort Belvoir.

When I returned from Vietnam in 1966, I found that the United States had been invaded by the British while I was away. The Beatles, the Dave Clark Five, Herman's Hermits, etc. They were all over the radio and TV. On my return this time, I learned that we had put astronauts on the moon, the whacko Manson family was killing people left and right in California, and some serious border clashes had erupted between the U.S.S.R. and China—and I was happy for both of them.

I had a lot to catch up on.

As glad as I was to again be living in my parents' home, my first priority was to get out of it. My mom was particularly upset when I told her I was moving out but I explained that I really needed to be in an apartment closer to Fort Belvoir. Even in the late 1960s, rush hour around the Nation's Capital was a beast.

Of course, that wasn't the only reason I wanted a place of my own. At almost twenty-nine, living with Mom and Dad was just a bad idea. I began apartment hunting and found a decent one bedroom apartment in a nice, new building on Duke Street in the city of Alexandria. It was a short ride down Duke Street to U. S. Route 1 then a reasonable drive south to the main gate of the fort. During my leave time, I bought some furniture, a TV, some curtains and stuff I thought every bachelor apartment needed, like a lava lamp.

I had been told by another officer living in my building that there were a lot of good looking girls in the building but every time I got on an elevator or looked left or right down the hallways, there was no one in sight. So, I now lived in Alexandria but found myself spending a lot of time back in Arlington where many of my high school buddies still lived. I did ask a pretty young lady who was an employee of my apartment building's rental office to go on a date with me and a relationship looked possible. Then, with the rental girl as my date, I hosted a party in my apartment that managed to get some complaints about noise and drunks in the hallways and elevators. After that, a relationship was not possible, and I was put on notice about further parties.

****

I had a friend of many years who did his military time as an officer in the Navy. Somewhere in his travels, he met a French girl named Josianne who came to the States to be with him. They got married and some other old friends and I helped move them into a little house they bought across the Potomac River in Maryland. This was before either of my trips to Vietnam. By the time I returned from my second Vietnam tour, Phil, my friend, had long ago finished his military obligation and had established himself in retail sales. He and Josianne lived in a much bigger house now and she had gotten herself a job working at the French Military Mission in Washington, D.C., part of the French Embassy. Josianne then became friends with another French girl named Janine who also worked at the Mission.

At the time, Janine was a recent widow and had a three-year-old son named Erik. He was named after a popular cigarillo of the same name because Janine thought it was a cool name. More about Janine and Erik later.

My month leave ended and I reported to my new duty station with the Combat Arms Branch of the Combined Arms Division of the Engineer School. The branch was run by an Infantry major and it was composed of captains and majors of the Infantry, Artillery and Armor Branches. The job was all about instructing Basic and Advance Course Engineer officer students in the roles and functions of the three combat arms branches.

Before anyone actually taught a class, they were given a lesson plan and instructed to put together a one hour class, preferably with training aides, which would be presented to a "Murder Board." The Murder Board was comprised of the Combined Arms Division chief, a lieutenant colonel, and selected members of the Combat Arms Branch. The purpose of this board was to listen to the class, ask questions, critique the class and instructor and basically determine if the presenter was good enough to present classes for Engineer Basic and Advance Course students. I know of no one who ever washed out for poor performance in front of the Murder Board.

Once I was cleared by the Board, I was assigned the topics that I would teach in both the Basic and Advance Courses. They ranged from a one hour class on Leadership for the Basic Course to a six hour block of instruction on Airborne Operations for the Advance Course.

When one wasn't teaching, one was expected to fine tune, update or otherwise improve his lesson plans. There was absolutely nothing difficult about this job. But regardless how many times I presented a class, I always stayed up late the night before rehearsing my material and finding places to insert some true stories or some humor.

Every few months, my name came up on the Staff Duty Officer (SDO) roster and I pulled a twenty-four hour stint on a Saturday or Sunday in the Post Headquarters. The job involved answering phones and notifying the appropriate people in the event of any problems.

In my personal life, I was dating the lovely Janine from the French Military Mission. She was a French citizen, however not one who was sent from France to do her job. Her whole family had emigrated from France in the '50s and lived in the U. S. I got in some trouble early in our relationship when I took Janine to a party with other guys from the Branch, and their wives or girlfriends. These guys were not wild drunks like the guys I had invited to my one and only party at my apartment; in fact, they were mostly married with children, or almost married like Janine and I. So it wasn't for getting drunk or wearing a lampshade on my head that I got in trouble. In this instance, I simply got into a conversation with some guys I worked with and did not pay sufficient attention to Janine. On our way home in the car, she lit into me for dropping her like, she said, "a bag of potato chips." I think she was reaching for "a sack of potatoes," but, as I so often have had to remind myself during our over forty years of marriage, English is not her native language.

We got past the bag of potato chips incident and a few weeks later, I asked her to marry me. The very next morning, I received a call in my apartment (I had called in sick that day) from a colonel from Infantry Branch. He said, "Major General Eugene Salet with NATO Headquarters in Brussels, Belgium, has asked to have you reassigned to NATO to serve as his aide-de-camp. Are you interested?" I told the good colonel, "Just last night I asked my girlfriend to marry me so, as much as I might otherwise have been interested, I have to decline the offer.

The colonel responded, "Good decision, Captain. Been there done that, know what I mean?"

I told him, "Yes, sir, I understand." End of conversation.

****

After the wedding, I had to get used to a lot of different things, like life with a four door sedan rather than a Corvette. My motorcycle was also gone. The toughest thing I had to get used to, however, was how easy it was for Erik to get me in trouble with his mom. Eventually, everything did get worked out and Erik, who is in his late forties today, is my legally adopted son and he fits in well with our other two sons. Chris, who I mentioned in the beginning of this story, is now a full colonel commanding a brigade in my old outfit, the 1st Cavalry Division. Our youngest son, Michael, started as a salesman and worked his way up to store manager in the Guitar Center chain before he left that to go into business for himself. He was doing well until the economy tanked and now he has a good job having something to do with "software." Erik got a job over Christmas with UPS while on holiday break from college his freshman year and liked it so much he quit school and became a driver. He can retire any time now but chooses not to.

A year after Janine and I married, I was promoted to major. Major is the lowest rank in a group of ranks called Field Grade Officers. These ranks are majors, lieutenant colonels and (full) colonels in pay grades 04, 05 and 06. Major is a rather crappy rank in that, except for the Aviation Branch, majors don't command anything. They are staff officers, executive officers, assistants, etc. I did get to wear a flying saucer hat with gold braid on the bill, called scrambled eggs, but other than that and a slight pay raise, nothing changed. I still taught the same classes to the same people.

One day I realized I had been at the Engineer School for almost three years and it was getting really old. However, there was one class I still enjoyed participating in. I was the lead instructor for the Basic Course's Survival, Escape and Evasion Course (SEE). This was an overnighter in the limited training grounds available at Fort Belvoir. Typically, this course, taught in all basic Army schools, starts off as a land navigation course, except between points A and B there are "aggressor forces" waiting to capture the students and deposit them in a POW camp. In that scenario, only the unlucky ones who get caught get the benefit of being intimidated and roughly treated by the aggressors who operate the camp. The lucky ones who don't get caught are denied that experience.

As the primary instructor for that course, I changed it so that all students in the exercise start by being deposited in the POW camp and suffer a degree of harsh treatment where they must decline to offer any more information than their name, rank and serial number. Then, a friendly partisan leads them to a weak spot in the camp perimeter and lets them escape. Those who are caught will again visit the camp, and those who don't, won't.

The fact is, we really didn't extend too much effort in recapturing anyone once they all had experienced being held in a hostile environment. The class took place outdoors in all types of weather and involved the use of real weapons firing blanks.

I still liked to be involved in this SEE class, but it only came around one time per Basic Course. Most of my other classes, such as "Airborne Operations" for example, didn't lend themselves much to change or innovation and were all pitched from behind the same podium in the same classroom. I was beginning to feel the urge to move along.

That being said, I did what most of my contemporaries would recommend against. I contacted Infantry Branch to check on any future plans for me and I found myself talking with the former Task Force advisor with the Vietnamese Airborne, then Major, now Colonel Norman Schwarzkopf. I asked if there was any movement on the horizon for me and he replied, "Coincidently, Rocky, there is."

He mentioned the advisory effort was still alive and well in Vietnam and said he'd get back to me. I never told Janine about this phone call and, if she reads my book, I guess I'll be in trouble again. Colonel Schwarzkopf called me a few days later and told me things were changing fast. The Vietnam advisory effort was no longer alive and well and was about to disappear due to the Paris peace talks. He said the best he could do for me was a thirteen month tour in Korea. I thought about that for a second, then said, "Fine, I'll take it." I added, "Colonel, I would like to do those thirteen months with the Second Infantry Division (2ID) on the DMZ." Colonel Schwarzkopf replied, "You'll be going over unassigned but don't worry, you'll be on a plane with a bunch of majors who don't want to go to the 2ID." He told me I'd have my orders quickly and wished me well.

Total time at Fort Belvoir was three years almost to the day.

Fourteen

The Land of the Morning Calm

T HE FLIGHT TO KOREA IN 1972 WAS AGAIN BY CONTRACT civilian airline. The cabin crew was friendly but not gushing like the crew who took us to Vietnam in 1968. Not for a minute do I doubt what Colonel Schwarzkopf said to me about flying to Korea on a plane full of officers who do not want to go to the 2ID. I believe that's what he thought would be the case. But, that's not the way it worked out.

We landed at an airbase near Seoul and were bused to the replacement depot at the U. S. Army Garrison at Yongson. This base housed the Headquarters of the Eighth U. S. Army (EUSA) commanded by a three star general. I still had high hopes of getting assigned to the division and accumulating some troop time as a major, even though I knew it would be as an executive officer or a staff officer at some level.

After a night sleeping in cots similar to those in Vietnam, I was interviewed by a staff sergeant who apparently was tasked with finding me a job. Before he asked me if I had any preference, I offered up my desire to go to the 2ID on the DMZ. His immediate reply was, "The division has all the majors it's going to get." That stung me somewhat. I saw myself in field gear around soldiers and getting acquainted with the tanks and armored personnel carriers I had avoided for so long which were assigned to the division. While the sergeant was saying something, I was thinking how he put it to me that the 2ID was not going to happen: "The division has all the majors it's going to get." That's not the same thing as, "The division has all the majors it is authorized." So the division was probably below authorized strength in many ranks and everywhere else in Eighth Army will be too.

Finally, I tuned the sergeant back in and he was talking about sending me for an interview with the Command G-1 to determine where they could best use me. I started wishing I had never made that call to Infantry Branch. When Colonel Schwarzkopf initially talked about the U. S. Advisory effort still being alive and well, I knew he was sending me back to Vietnam, and I was okay with that. The diversion to Korea would have been alright if I could have landed in the 2ID. Now I was beginning to miss Fort Belvoir and my lesson plans and, of course, Janine.

The next day, I made myself look sharp in my Class A uniform as I walked the few blocks to EUSA Headquarters for my interview. I would be interviewed by a Lieutenant Colonel William Sewell, Chief of the Personnel Services Division. He was a pleasant man and made me feel welcome. Too bad LTC Gibney didn't take some lessons from him. He told me that due to Vietnam, the entire command was understrength.

The message there was, everybody in the command has to work harder with less. He added, however, the anticipated draw down from Vietnam should result in a correction to the command's understrength status. Not in time, I thought, to get me a slot in the 2ID. LTC Sewell had extracts from my personnel record in front of him and asked me some general questions, which I answered. Then he advised me that the Army was taking a hard look at the state of race relations in our ranks and he was establishing a Human Relations Branch in his division. He asked me if I would have any objection to being assigned to this branch.

Was this a trick question? Just before I left Fort Belvoir, the Combined Arms Division announced it would be starting a Race Relations/Equal Opportunity block of instruction to be presented to Engineer Basic and Advanced Courses. So, the thing about the Army taking a hard look at race relations was not BS. But now, how should I answer his question? If I objected, I might be perceived to be a racist and where the hell would I end up? So, I answered, "No sir, I have no objection to being assigned to the Human Relations Branch."

So, my first real assignment as a field grade officer was as an RR/EO guy. Well, at least I found a home. Shortly after I agreed to this assignment, I met my branch chief, LTC Awtrey, a white guy; the senior NCO, SFC Schwartz, a white guy; as a major, I was the next senior person in the branch, a white guy. I met branch member Lieutenant Ben Taylor, a black guy; an RR/EO NCO, SSG Gaillard, a black guy; and the secretary, Mrs. Kim, a Korean national.

In the course of my Korean assignment, I would be the primary author of the EUSA Race Relations/Equal Opportunity Plan. It wasn't an easy assignment. I personally carried the draft to every principal staff officer in the EUSA Headquarters seeking their approval. This was very difficult because everyone found something about the Plan they didn't like. When I got it past the principal staff officers, the Plan then had to climb its way up through the chief of staff, the deputy commanding general and, finally, the commanding general. This was not an easy climb.

The first attempt came back to me with light blue ink markings indicating things the chief of staff had a problem with. When the chief's issues were resolved and the Plan made its way to the deputy's desk, it then came back to me with red ink indicating the deputy's issues with the Plan. When the deputy was satisfied, my Plan went to the desk of the commanding general, Lieutenant General John H. Michaelis. Shortly afterwards, it made its way back to me with numerous markings in green ink. The lesson for me there was light blue ink was reserved for the chief of staff, red ink was the mark of the deputy and green ink was reserved for the CG.

Ultimately, the EUSA RR/EO Plan was blessed by everyone. It took me damn near the whole year to get it done but I did feel like I accomplished something. But, compared to the responsibilities I had as a captain in Vietnam, I was not feeling too impressed with being Field Grade.

It turns out that I finished the RR/EO project just in time because, although I wasn't expecting it, I had been selected to attend the Armed Forces Staff College in Norfolk, Virginia. This is the equivalent of the Army's Command and General Staff College in Fort Leavenworth, Kansas, but it lies in the bailiwick of the Joint Chiefs of Staff. The student body would include officers of each of the services.

Only when I saw the selection list did I recall that somewhere in the past, I submitted a Preference Statement asking that, when I become eligible for mid-level schooling, I prefer to go to the Armed Forces Staff College in Norfolk rather than C&GS in Kansas. So far in my career, the Army had given me everything I'd asked for.

Korea is known as the Land of the Morning Calm. This title was given to Korea by an emperor of the Ming Dynasty many years ago; I have no idea why. I mean this with no disrespect to the Korean people (I love bulgogi and even kimchi) but to me it was the land of the morning yawn. Pushing paper was painful drudgery. There was no excitement, no adrenalin rush, nothing but getting up in the morning to sit behind a desk and fool around with paper and then walking that paper around trying to get important people to sign off on it. I looked forward to my attendance at the Armed Forces Staff College (AFSC). Janine still had her job at the French Military Mission and we agreed that I would get a BOQ room on the Norfolk Naval Base and come home on weekends.

Fifteen

Armed Forces Staff College
and Beyond

I VIEWED MY UPCOMING FIVE MONTHS AT THE AFSC as a reward for enduring eleven months at EUSA. Students were organized into small, manageable groups called seminars. Each seminar had a pretty equal number from the Army, Air Force and Navy. We didn't have a Marine but we did have a Canadian Army officer. For the next five months, we would attend lectures and engage in computer assisted war games involving the entire world. As we got to know each other, we learned that almost to a man, our Air Force brothers who were pilots had all been guests at the Hanoi Hilton. Everyone treated them with respect.

I was assigned housing at the naval base BOQ. It was a grand old rooming house complete with a contingent of Filipino Navy enlisted men who served dinner, carried drinks from the bar to us, maintained our rooms to include making the beds, and also provided a morning wake up service. I imagined this was pretty much the way things were on board an aircraft carrier.

We found ourselves, willing or not, on seminar softball teams with a schedule of competition which would reveal a championship team right about the time we graduated.

While we were learning, we actually had some fun. Almost every one of us in the BOQ was a geographic bachelor with a family elsewhere. Mine was an easy four hour ride away, which I made every Friday after class. The most fun night of the week was Monday when we all crowded into the TV lounge for Monday Night Football. While we laughed and cheered, the stewards were busy shuttling drinks into the lounge. After one particularly exciting Monday night game, a prankster went up and down the hall around 0200 hours knocking on doors and saying, in his best Filipino accent, "Eees seees o'clock, eees time to get up." No one ever admitted to doing that and it didn't happen again.

When I would come home on weekends, Janine and I had some serious business to talk about. Specifically, with a minimum of fifteen years of service with the French government, Janine would be able to retire, not with a pension, but with a lump sum of cash which was not insignificant in the mid-'70s. She had twelve years on the job. After graduation, would I dare ask for another three years in the Washington area? What was the alternative? Probably a three year tour in Germany by myself. The cash looked good to both of us, but I felt sure Infantry Branch wasn't going to let me get away with it this time. I would find out soon enough because time was rolling along and it wouldn't be long before the Army, Navy, Air Force and Marine (there were a few Marines in the class, just not in my seminar) assignment people would be there to help us with our careers.

When that day arrived, I decided I would tell the Infantry Branch guys what I wanted to do and why. With Vietnam pretty much over, promotions were going to slow down and I figured to be in the sucking rank of major for several years. Enough years, I thought, that I could do two or even three more in the Washington area and still have time to be a battalion XO or S-3 somewhere in the U. S. Army.

The young Airborne Ranger LTC who had my file got to the point: "Major, this is the year for Europe," he said.

I replied, "Sir, I need to go back to the Washington area for another three years. It's a financial matter."

"Well," he replied, "that financial matter is going to mess up your career. You need to be in Germany, not next year but right now."

"I understand the D.C. area isn't the best move for me, but that is what I am asking for." Looking like a man who just lost all his patience, the LTC turned over the piece of paper he held pertaining to me and slammed it face down on a table. He said, "You write me a statement on the backside of this paper stating you have been advised that you should be going to Europe, but you still want to go to D. C., and sign it, and I will get you back to the D. C. area."

That's exactly what I did and handed him back the paper. Then he said to me, "Don't be surprised when you are not selected for battalion command." End of conversation.

Before graduation, I received my orders. I was being assigned to the Army Staff, specifically to the Office of the Chief of Information (OCINFO), Department of the Army, Washington, D. C. Technically, the exact location was The Pentagon in Arlington, Virginia. I was okay with that and Janine was happy. The only thing nagging at me was, over all the years that I had lived in Arlington, as I drove home from downtown over the 14th Street Bridge at 10:00 or 11:00 o'clock at night, I noticed that all the lights in all the offices in the Pentagon were still on and the parking lot was half full of cars.

Sixteen

The Five Sided Sweat Shop

A GOOD THING HAPPENED BEFORE I EVEN REPORTED to The Pentagon for duty. When I first started the AFSC, there was a gas shortage and stations with gas were selling only to drivers with license plates ending in odd or even numbers depending on the day of the week. About mid-way through school, the states got serious about the gas shortage and began lowering speed limits to conserve fuel. We went from a 70 mph limit to 55 mph, and this was vigorously enforced. The Defense Department made its contribution to gas conservation by withdrawing all individual POV parking permits thereby forcing the workforce either into car pools or onto public transportation. The reason this was a good thing was that every one, unless they planned to spend the night, had to be gone no later than the last public bus going in their direction. Burning the midnight oil was now a thing of the past, except in real emergencies.

That was the only good thing that happened. I was assigned to the Administrative Services Division and became responsible for the steno pool and the like. Working for me were tenured civilians who long ago determined how fast they were going to work and when they were taking breaks. The division chief, LTC Stewart, was a good guy and did what he could to keep morale high. That being said, the job really stunk.

My desk was by an open door beyond which was a hallway that lead to the C Ring. At every opportunity, I bailed out through this door and explored the building. I found the Army Library and spent as much time there as I could. I could say I hated my job, but what job? The civilians did their thing without me. One day, I was summoned to the office of the Deputy Chief of Information, a brigadier general. When I walked into his office, he had a handful of paper towels and was wiping a stream of water coming down his wall from above. He yelled, "Get some of these towels and help me out!" Without knowing what I was wiping, I started wiping. A secretary had notified building maintenance and a cleanup crew was inbound. When they arrived, they reported that the private crapper of the three-star above the brigadier overflowed. I'm thinking to myself, "Why the hell didn't I go to Germany?"

While I was in Admin, I made friends with the civilian who was the Chief of the Plans and Policy Division (PPD). He was the equivalent of an LTC and old enough to be a senior one of those, but we got along well. One day he told me he was about to have a vacancy in PPD and asked if I was interested. I had been there long enough to know a little something about all the OCINFO jobs but I asked for more detail. He said I would be one of the "Action Officers" assigned to major acquisition projects. "It will be your job to come up with every possible question the press could ask about a new acquisition and the selection process leading to that acquisition," he said. "Then, after you have developed all the questions, you will get in bed, so to speak, with the project managers and get the answers to those questions. The purpose of this, of course is so an Army spokesperson, at the unveiling of this new item, is able to answer any question, without hesitation, the press might have about the hardware and the selection process."

He continued, "Right now we are testing three prototype main battle tanks and we will be selecting a winner in the near future. This project, in fact, can be your first if you come to PPD."

I knew about the tank project, which involved two American entries, one from Chrysler and one from General Motors, and a third tank, the Leopard, from West Germany. I thought that any job was better than the one I had and I accepted his offer. He greased the skids with the two-star Chief of Information and I became an "Action Officer."

As I was making this transition a couple of other things happened. One was the name of the agency changed. The new name was the now the Office of the Chief of Public Affairs (OCPA). Supposedly, this change was necessary because the public frequently called the agency asking for phone numbers or other bits of "information" such as, "What's playing tonight at the Fort Myer movie theater?"

The other was that the Army launched a new Officer Personnel Management System (OPMS). In theory, each officer would be allowed to pick a secondary specialty, a different Military Occupational Specialty (MOS), and this officer would then serve in his secondary MOS when not in his primary MOS. It sounded good to me and when I had my chance to pick a secondary specialty, I picked Military Police.

In the meantime, I was still in the information field. But picking MPs caused me to look higher. At the age of thirty-three I submitted an application to the FBI for the position of Special Agent. Then, one day, I got a call from an FBI agent who identified himself as an applicant screener and we made an appointment for me to meet with him at the Washington field office located in the Old Post Office Building in downtown D.C.

Agent John House was a distinguished silver haired man, perhaps ten years older than me. Having come from The Pentagon, I was in my uniform and Agent House asked if I planned to stay in the Reserves if I were hired by the Bureau. I told him I'd like to, but then he told me the Bureau preferred its agents not have any military obligations. In that case, I told him I would not stay in the Army Reserve. After some polite chit chat, he leveled with me. "Accountants and lawyers are always preferred candidates for Special Agent and, to be perfectly honest, minorities and women will also be in front of you." We shook hands and, although he told me I would remain on the list of possible candidates, he thought my chances were extremely slim.

After that, I also looked into joining the Secret Service but I couldn't get by some personnel clerk who told me I'd have to leave the military before I could even apply for the Service. Then, I pictured myself sitting in a rocking chair outside Mamie Eisenhower's bedroom door in Gettysburg, PA, and decided to forget about the Secret Service.

Following the discovery of FBI "Black Bag" jobs and some other questionable stuff, it became policy that FBI Special Agents must retire at age fifty-five. On my 35th birthday, I received a letter from the FBI thanking me for my interest in the Bureau and informing me that I was no longer eligible for the position of Special Agent.

I liked my job with PPD much better than the admin job, but I was still in the information field, an occupational specialty I would have never picked for myself. Still, I was making some friends. I had a counterpart in Public Affairs in the Office of the Secretary of Defense (OSD). We coordinated on a number of projects and I liked working with him. But my PPD "Action Officer" job was sometimes like pulling teeth.

The crusty colonels and occasional brigadier generals who were picked as project managers were a tough bunch. They understood the need for an Army spokesperson to be able to answer any and all questions about why one piece of hardware was selected over another, and they would find the answers to my questions, but they didn't want to give those answers to me. I tried to explain that it could be my boss, the Army Chief of Public Affairs, who might be the spokesman these questions were directed at and, gradually and grudgingly, I did get answers to most of my questions.

Besides the XM-1 tank, several other major acquisitions were given to me to work with while I was in PPD. Then, out of the blue, I took a call at my desk one day and the caller identified himself as LTC Jones from Military Police Branch. He stated, "We are looking at your file and see that you have completed several military police correspondence courses," which I had. And then, to my surprise, he said, "We also see from a battery of tests you took as a young lieutenant that you have an aptitude for learning a foreign language." I didn't remember taking any such test but I guess I had or they wouldn't be telling me that. Then came the question, "How would you like to study Russian for a year at DLI in Monterey, California, and then go to Berlin where you will be the Special Operations Officer in the Provost Marshal's Office? In that job you will deal, on behalf of the Berlin Command, with the Soviets on matters of U. S. access into East Berlin and through East Germany."

I was stunned, but I said, "May I discuss this with my wife tonight and call you back tomorrow?" The reply was, "Yes, certainly, but do call me back tomorrow, one way or the other." I assured him I would.

Janine had only one year left in order to reach fifteen years with the French. I could see me going to Monterey by myself for a year and, by the time I graduated (if I graduated), we could go to Berlin as a family. I didn't know how much aptitude I really had for learning a foreign language but I guess I was going to find out.

Janine loved the part about going to Berlin, and the next day I called MP Branch and told LTC Jones I wanted the Berlin job. The next time I saw my OSD friend, I told him about the call from MP Branch. Instead of slapping me on the back and saying, "Congratulations," he appeared disappointed and told me he too was leaving and he had recommended me to his boss to replace him on the OSD staff. I was flattered but, although I would be working at a higher level, I would still be in the information business.

I'm sure I will prefer Berlin, I thought. *All I have to do is not flunk out of the Russian language course.*

The Pentagon was not a pleasant place to work. Every assigned task was due yesterday and everything you have almost completed becomes no longer important. I will not forget that just being in that building caused me to actively seek another line of work. Majors are a rare commodity in the building, with the overwhelming number of "Action Officers" being lieutenant colonels or colonels. That meant my chances of coming back there were probably good. A twenty-year career was starting to make more sense to me than a thirty.

Seventeen

Ich Bin Ein Berliner

G ETTING THROUGH THE RUSSIAN LANGUAGE COURSE was probably the most challenging thing I have ever accomplished. Our language class was small, only around twelve of us. As a major, I was the ranking student so I became the class leader. There was an MP captain in the class, Dan Doherty, and he was also going to the U. S. Army, Berlin (USAB) and the Provost Marshal's Office (PMO). He was being trained as my back-up and my eventual replacement because I should be promoted to LTC about half-way through the Berlin assignment.

Dan, a Navy lieutenant and me were studying Russian so we could communicate with real Russians. The enlisted soldiers in the class were going to use their language skills sitting between a set of earphones listening in on Russian conversations. There were two FBI agents in the class also and I had no idea what they were going to do with their Russian. I was glad my family did not accompany me to Monterey because I spent all my time studying. We probably would have gotten divorced.

As a geographic bachelor, I was assigned a room in the old BOQ which, again, was a cinderblock room with a bathroom between rooms to be shared with the person in the next room. There were a lot of empty rooms in this old BOQ and the room on the other side of my bathroom was unassigned.

That being the case, I arranged for one of the two FBI agents in the class, a real bachelor, to move into it. My FBI roommate was smarter than me and when we weren't in class, I was studying my ass off and he was sitting on his watching TV. But, I persevered and passed the course. I was advised by one of our instructors that I was an oddball in that I spoke Russian better than I comprehended. Apparently, it was usually the other way around.

We got to Berlin in late September, 1977. We had just settled into a military apartment building and had invited the MP captain I was replacing and his wife to join us for dinner. He had no training in the Russian language and I was curious how he did this job, but I never asked. I also never asked what happened to the last guy in this job who *did* speak Russian.

No sooner had our guests arrived than I got a phone call telling me the Russians wanted to see the U. S. representative and a car was coming to pick me up.

There were three Allied checkpoints between the Federal Republic of Germany, the German Democratic Republic (FRG/GDR) and East Berlin. Checkpoint Alpha was at Helmstedt, West Germany. Allied travelers to West Berlin processed through this checkpoint. Then, 110 miles up the autobahn, at the beginning of the Allied Sectors of Berlin sat Checkpoint Bravo. Arriving Allied travelers checked in at Checkpoint Bravo. Then, of course, there was the third and most famous, Checkpoint Charlie on Friedrichstrasse between the Allied Sectors and East Berlin. Checkpoint Bravo was an important link in communications between the Soviets and the Allies.

When the Soviets wanted to see one of the Allied representatives they handed something we called "The Plaque" to an inbound Allied traveler of the same nationality as the representative they wanted to see. This traveler was instructed by the Soviets to present The Plaque to the Gendarmes, the Royal MPs or the U. S. MPs at Bravo. The MPs receiving The Plaque would then call their PMO which would result in the appropriate representative going to the Soviet checkpoint at Drewitz, GDR, about half a mile away.

So on that evening of September, 1977, I left Janine with our guests and proceeded to pick up The Plaque at Checkpoint Bravo and return it to my Soviet counterparts. This would be my first meeting with Pod Polcovnik (LTC) Volkov, Mayor (Major) Tshintsov and later, assorted duty captains I would come to know over the next eighteen months. The purpose of this visit was to take custody of an errant American traveler and his family who managed to get off the authorized corridor and, according to LTC Volkov, "violated the sovereign territory of the German Democratic Republic." I had been told earlier by the Provost Marshal that this was not uncommon so don't apologize for it.

It was actually not hard to make such a mistake. There were three clover leaf turns Allied travelers had to successfully negotiate to get to West Berlin. They were stacked up on the Berlin end of the corridor at twenty-three, seventeen and nine miles from the Allied Sectors. Travelers were all briefed on autobahn travel and given a map showing the turns as well as flash cards to communicate, if necessary, with East Germans or Russians. The flash cards for East Germans simply demanded that a Soviet officer be brought to their location. The long drive through East Germany can be a white knuckle experience, especially for first time travelers. And, the East Germans helped already nervous Allied drivers make wrongs turns by frequently switching the overhead signs at these turns. Then they would lay in wait for someone to "violate the sovereign territory of the GDR." After they make their stop, they would detain these unfortunate people until it was time, apparently at their discretion, to lead the lost travelers to the Russians at Drewitz. The Soviets then would send The Plaque to Checkpoint Bravo asking for the appropriate Allied representative. When the Allies wanted to see the Russians, however, we simply hopped in our vehicles and drove out to their checkpoint.

Early on, I was advised that, although the British and the French actually socialized with the Russians at their checkpoint after business has been conducted, we Americans were strictly business.

Let me just say, I didn't behave towards the Russians like I had a stick up my butt. They were cordial enough with me and I treated them the same way. We were cordial even when we were delivering protests to each other, which I had to do from time to time, and so did they. My first protest came when incoming Allied travelers reported that the Soviets were flying the East German flag in their checkpoint on some East German holiday. This was a violation of the Four-Power Agreements about the status of Berlin and East Germany. When it was protest time, I would be notified by the Office of the United States Minister to Berlin (USBER) that a protest was being formulated and, when finished, it would be brought to the PMO for me to deliver to the Soviets. But first, of course, I had to use my trusty dictionary and translate it from English into Russian. The protests were always delivered to me late in the day because, I'm sure, they had to be blessed by the U. S. Ambassador in Bonn. At this point, let me be clear that the United States Department of State, through the U. S. Minister in Berlin, really ran the American Sector of the city, not the military.

I was pleased that my Soviet counterparts and I didn't get emotionally involved in the protests. During my tenure, there were

Author *(far left)* standing in front of a picture of Lenin at a Soviet checkpoint just outside of Berlin. Also pictured *(left to right)*: The author's Russian counterpart, Lieutenant Colonel Volkov; Major Dan Doherty from the Provost Marshal's office; and Major Tshintsov, circa 1980

Author during his time with the Fairfax County Sheriff's Office. The three stripes on his sleeves indicates his rank is that of major, circa the early 1990s

A 2004 photo of the author dressed for a reunion of Vietnamese paratroopers in Washington, D.C. "I was still able to fit into the actual uniform issued to me in 1965!"

Author (*center*) with former Vietnamese paratroopers at their 2004 reunion in Washington, D.C.

Three Angry Skipper 6's (*left to right*): Buddy Garner, who passed D 2/8 to the author; the author; and Ed Livingston, who took over the company from the author. Fort Benning reunion, 2009

Author and his wife Janine visiting New River Gorge, West Virgina, summer of 2014

no threats of closing the corridor to Allied traffic or any disruption to our daily business. My assessment of "my" Russians was that they were soldiers, like me, and not political commissars.

In addition to responding to The Plaque or delivering protests, my presence was also required at the Soviet checkpoint for out and in processing of U. S. military convoys with eight or more vehicles. Smaller convoys could process themselves through the checkpoint. There were some petty Cold War politics played during these convoys. For example, a simple typographical error on our convoy travel orders could delay movement of the convoy until the order was retyped. Whiteout was not allowed. So, the convoy waited while another order was prepared and brought to the checkpoint.

Another game the Soviets played was while taking a headcount of soldiers in the back of deuce-and-a-half trucks in a convoy, they would step up on the bumper of the truck to do so. It was my job to remind them that touching the vehicle was not permitted and, if necessary, I would have our soldiers stand to be counted. I'm sure "my" Russians were told to do this.

I became an expert on the subject of Occupation law and Allied access to and through the East. There were actually a dozen crossing points between East and West Berlin and the Allies maintained the right to use any of them. The Allies chose, however, to require our people to cross into the East only at Checkpoint Charlie. This was so we knew who went into East Berlin and who to look for if they didn't come back out. As far as the other crossing points, we conducted what we called probes. Wearing our uniforms, we would make a show of driving, walking or taking the subway through the other crossing points, strutting right past the GDR border police.

The Allied policy on East Berlin was that it was still the Soviet Sector of greater Berlin and we answered only to Soviet authorities while in their sector. The Soviet policy was that there was no longer an occupation and East Berlin was the capital of the GDR. In line with their view, there were rarely any Soviet authorities visible at any crossing point into East Berlin, including Checkpoint Charlie.

The Allied Control Authority building in West Berlin, was the last place where Soviets, in this case air traffic controllers, worked with their American, British and French counterparts. There were three authorized air corridors through which American, British and French flag airlines could use to enter or depart West Berlin. No other civilian aircraft were authorized to fly in these corridors. There was a northern, central and southern corridor. When the U.S., British or French air controller in the ACA building was notified that a civilian aircraft from his country was coming to West Berlin, he would write the flight information on a card and give it to his Soviet counterpart. The Soviet air controller would then rubber stamp the card, "Safety of Flight Not Guaranteed," although they did communicate this flight information to their air defenses around the city. Then they would go back to throwing darts, playing ping pong or whatever else they were doing between flights.

As the Special Operations Officer for the Provost Marshal, I had a Physical Security Section under my control. This section was made up of two highly motivated senior NCOs whose job was to continuously inspect USAB arms rooms to ensure they were protected with anti-intrusion devices and met stringent military security standards. With three Infantry battalions and a tank company in the Berlin brigade, these NCOs stayed busy. But I often heard them complain about something called the West Berlin Hunting Club and its arms storage facility which, I understood, had never passed an inspection and never could. They told me the club was where prominent West Berlin citizens stored their hunting rifles because, under Occupation law, they were not allowed to possess privately owned firearms in their homes. I was, therefore, aware of the problem but not really concerned with it. My relationship with the physical security NCOs was like my relationship had been with my communications NCOs back in the 82nd Airborne. I wasn't all that interested.

Over the year and a half that I was the MP Special Operations Officer, promotions from the lieutenant colonels' list were moving towards my number. When I actually made LTC, it was clear that Captain, now Major Dan Doherty would replace me as the Special Operations Officer. What wasn't clear was where I was going.

I got my first hint one day when a colonel from the U.S. Army, Europe (USAEUR) Inspector General's (IG) office in Heidelberg called me at work and asked me when I would be reporting in. I told the colonel I knew nothing about such an assignment but I certainly would look into it. In my current job, my boss was the Provost Marshal. But on matters of the Occupation and access, I answered to a different position, LTC Jim Miller, who was the Deputy Chief of Staff for Political/Military Affairs (DCS, Pol/Mil). He was the military link with the State Department. I first asked LTC Ken Alderson, the Provost Marshal, if he knew anything about a transfer to Heidelberg, and he did not. Then I asked LTC Miller if he knew anything about the Heidelberg assignment, and he did. He told me that he was working on a transfer for himself to the Allied staff, Berlin, and he planned to recommend me to be his replacement as DCS, Pol/Mil.

The part about me replacing LTC Miller was absolutely fine with me. In that job, LTC Miller oversaw Occupation and access matters and he knew the governing regulations well; however, I not only knew the governing regulations and Occupation law as well as he did, I was also a practitioner of these regulations and four-power agreements. I dealt mano-a-mano with the Russians. I performed the crossing point probes and stared down the GDR Border police. I was the one dispatched down the autobahn when an American traveler had an accident or incident with East Germans or Russians. I really wanted this job.

The part that disturbed me was the implication that if Miller didn't get his transfer, I'd be off to Heidelberg. But there was a new CG in town with a new chief of staff and when the chief learned my staying in the command depended on LTC Miller's transfer, they transferred him to Heidelberg. I became the new DCS, Pol/Mil and was promoted immediately afterwards.

The new C G was Major General Calvert P. Benedict, that same highly decorated and sharp LTC who took command of the 1/505, 82nd Airborne, just as I was leaving. His chief of staff was Colonel Robert Spiller, whom I had never heard of, but others in the command had. It seems he had a reputation similar to Colonel Murphy of the 82nd who once famously told me, "Fuck your nose, Lieutenant. You're on the track team."

****

Immediately after my promotion and new status as the DCS, Pol/Mil, I moved from the PMO into an office in the U.S. Command Headquarters on Clayallee (Goering's former Luftwaffe headquarters, which had a bit part in the movie "Inglorious Bastards"), and my family and I moved from a duplex house where "regular" majors and captains lived, into a "requisitioned" mansion walking distance from my office. (FYI: "Requisitioned" houses in the Western sectors of Berlin were houses that were not legally claimed after the war. The previous owners either died during the war, possibly in concentration camps or the actual fighting, or just abandoned them. These were generally very large and nice houses and were assigned to higher ranking people in the U.S, British and French sectors.)

Staff meetings in the headquarters were held inside the "bubble." The bubble was a clear Plexiglas room inside a larger room that was bug proof. To my surprise, one of the first items on the agenda at my first meeting in the bubble was the arms storage room of the West Berlin Hunting Club. This was the substandard building used to hold the hunting rifles of West Berlin elite, and they had not been happy hunters for a long time. General Benedict said, "There must be some way to get this building opened so these guys can hunt." I raised my hand and said, "Sir, all we have to do is get this building off the U.S. Command Property Book and reassign it to USBER. Then it won't have to meet Army standards for an Arms Room." Stunned silence. No one said anything for a while, and then Colonel Spiller asked, "Can this be done?" And one of the full colonels on the staff replied, "Yes it can, and I will coordinate with USBER to get it done." Then the U.S. Minister said, "We will be happy to assume control over the Hunting Club Structure.

Thus, a very long and aggravating problem for the U. S. Command, Berlin, evaporated. Had I paid attention to this situation when my Physical Security NCOs were talking about it, I could have proposed this solution well over a year earlier. But then, I would have proposed the solution to the Provost Marshal or to LTC Miller and one of them would have gotten the credit. It was better this way!

My remaining eighteen months were wonderful. Since the Berlin Army command was only a two star billet, a LTC was a big man in town. And I had made a friend in Colonel Spiller that made my job as one of his principal assistants one of the best jobs I ever had in the military, to rival being Angry Skipper 6.

But again it was time for Janine and I to have a talk. She had told me many times that it was her dream to open and run a retail jewelry and gift shop. I knew I faced the prospect of maybe going back to The Pentagon or some similarly joyless place so we agreed that, one more time, I'd ask to go back to the D. C. area, but this time it was to do three more years and retire. We still owned our home in the Falls Church section of Fairfax County. *My last three years may again suck but I'll help her get her store up and running and then I'll write a book while her store pays our way.* We shook on it and that was the deal.

Eighteen

The U. S. Army Military District of Washington
(HQ, USAMDW)

MY TOUR IN BERLIN WAS COMING TO A CLOSE. I sent Janine and the boys home ahead of me to get the two oldest registered in school and to move back into our Falls Church home. I loved my assignment in Berlin but time was almost up and things were going to change anyway.

Colonel Spiller had reached the maximum time he could serve on active duty and was being forced to retire, even though General Benedict wanted to keep him. I worked for that man for a year and a half and I really liked him, and I can say with confidence that the feeling was mutual. In short order, Colonel Spiller's replacement arrived. I moved out of our big house and into the BOQ counting down the days until I was back home. Then, a complication arose. In my position as DCS, Pol/Mil, I also served as a special magistrate under Occupation law. In this position, I was one of a few who could be called by Army criminal investigators to obtain a warrant to search the premises of any American suspect anywhere in the American Sector.

I shared this authority with the two-star, the one-star and the chief of staff. Now, if you were an Army criminal investigator and wanted a search warrant, particularly at 2:00 am, who would you call—the two-star, the one-star the chief, or me? They all called me, of course—at any time, day or night!

After they articulated their probable cause, and if I deemed it sufficient, I granted the search warrant. One subject of a warrant I granted was going on trial soon and he or his defense attorney wanted me present in court so my departure was delayed. My replacement as DCS, Pol/Mil was on board already so all I had to do was hang out and help him learn the job. After a few days hanging out, I was informed that the defendant's trial had been delayed. My situation then became, I could go home but I would be brought back for the trial. I made all my travel arrangements and just before I left Berlin, the defendant took a plea and there would not be a trial at all. I flew home to Virginia.

Once back in the Washington Metropolitan Area, I was assigned to the Office of the Deputy Chief of Staff for Operations (ODCSOPS), HQ, USAMDW, a high visibility command known as a "no mistake command." My new boss was Colonel Lamar Stroud. He welcomed me to his shop and told me, "Based on your experience as a Deputy Provost Marshal in Berlin, I am assigning you as Chief of the Law Enforcement Branch."

Under me were a driver, an NCO and two captains, but no troops. I was the officer in charge of all command level operations involving the Military Police and for these operations, I tasked the Provost Marshals of Fort Myer, Fort McNair and Davison Army Airfield to cough up the warm bodies from their MP detachments to perform these operations. If I thought pulling answers out of project managers when I was an IO at The Pentagon was tough, pulling MPs away from these Provost Marshals was equally so. And, when those same Provost Marshals found out that my basic branch was Infantry and I was not "a real MP," cooperation got tougher. But, despite all their pissing and moaning, I would ultimately get the number of MPs I needed for a specific operation. During my three years as the chief of the Law Enforcement Branch, I directed MP support for the first inauguration of President Ronald Reagan. This support actually involved two battalions of MPs on loan to MDW to augment local police around the entire Capital Beltway, while MDW Military Police supported the Secret Service protecting VIPs. Another high visibility event was support for the Secret Service, the U. S. Park and the D.C. Metropolitan Police during the funeral of General Omar Bradley, with services in the Washington Cathedral and burial in Arlington National Cemetery. MDW MPs supported the Secret Service in Arlington Cemetery every time a foreign head of state or, for that matter, our own president, as they laid wreaths at the Tomb of the Unknowns. MDW MPs also supported the U. S. Marshal's Service as they transported would be presidential assassin John Hinckley from the brig at Quantico Marine Base to Fort McNair for his drive into D. C. for hearings on his attempted assassination of President Reagan, and the same for former CIA officer Edwin Wilson, convicted of selling arms to Libya. My MDW assignment was very busy and the three years went by fast.

****

In the beginning of 1983, I began to rethink my decision to retire. I would be in the zone of consideration for promotion to full colonel soon and I saw no reason why I wouldn't get that promotion. The rules at that time, however, were that one must remain in a rank at least three years in order to retire in that rank.

So, I would wait a year to get promoted and then stay in the Army three more.

I knew Janine would go ahead with plans for her store, regardless of my decision. She had already been scouting for a good location. I decided to stick to our agreement and retire effective 1 July 1983.

Another consideration in making a final decision to retire was that I was not very happy about the pettiness or silliness in this "no mistake command." I served under three different major general commanders of MDW during my three years there. One of them, it was well known, would have a meltdown if he received a clipped together bunch of papers with the long part of the paper clip on top of the stack and the short part of the clip on the back. It was so well-known that I don't recall it ever happening while I was there.

Another commander, despite the many valid definitions of the word "render," believed it had solely to do with butchering an animal and anyone who used that word otherwise would, as a minimum, have his paper thrown in the trash.

In addition to quirky MDW commanders, the posts of Fort Myer and Fort McNair provided elegant housing for many three and four star generals and admirals who worked in the National Capitol region. These flag officers, and their wives, often had comments or suggestions regarding MDW operations. In one particular case, the spouse of a flag officer told her husband that she was offended by the lackadaisical salute and wave given to her as she drove through a gate at Fort Myer. Additionally, she felt that this particular MP's appearance in uniform was sloppy. This resulted in a study which, despite objections by many, placed the sharpest, handsomest, tallest, fittest MPs on gate duty with actual policing on post left to the shortest and dumpiest.

In looking back over twenty years of soldiering, my years of service as a field grade officer, with the exception of those three years in Berlin, were nowhere near as challenging and rewarding as my years as a company grade officer.

Nineteen

The Gift Shop and the Sheriff

I ELECTED TO TAKE MY ACCRUED SIXTY DAYS LEAVE before I actually retired from the Army. Janine had found a location for her store, "The 14 Karat Gift Shop," and signed a five year lease. Now we needed to bring in store fixtures and merchandise. We had a substantial safe to hold the jewelry and we had already acquired showcases, shelf units and other fixtures, mainly from other similar businesses that had closed. Her line of 14 Karat jewelry came mostly from her brother's factory in Rhode Island. Additionally, brother Bobby arranged for her to carry some heavier, cast jewelry such as necklaces and pendants. Besides the gold jewelry, she carried lots of cutesy things as well as a line of greeting cards.

My efforts to outfit the store, as well as opening it in the morning to be relieved by Janine around noon, caused me to forget all about the very nice ceremony and pass-in-review held the end of each month at Fort Myer for soldiers retiring at the end of that month. Missing the ceremony had no effect on my actual retirement and I was officially retired on July 1, 1983.

I actually hated being in the store by myself. I was uncomfortable with all the breakables surrounding me. One day, a lady asked to see an angel figurine that was quite expensive. My hands were slightly trembling as I slid open the display case door and just about the time I almost had the angel free of the case, I caught a wing on the showcase door and broke it off. I asked the lady, "Did you want this with one wing or two?" She made for the door.

Since the main item in this store was 14K jewelry, Janine insisted that I wear a gold bracelet and chain around my neck when I worked there, which I also hated. One day a woman, obviously from the country, looked at my jewelry and remarked, "Where I come from, men don't wear that stuff." I fought the temptation to tell her to go back where she came from, and after she left, I took off the bracelet and chain and never wore them again.

****

Writing a book, as I thought I might do, was really not in the cards. The drop from active duty pay to retired pay was significant and it was quickly clear that I had to find a job. Most police departments, and I had looked at this when I was despondent at The Pentagon, were not hiring officers over a certain age. My brother Bill was a Fairfax County police officer and he told me that the County Sheriff's Office did not have any age conditions for employment. If a candidate were otherwise eligible and could pass a background check and get a Class A physical exam, the Sheriffs' Office would hire them, provided there were job vacancies. In most counties in Virginia, the Sheriff is the chief law enforcement officer. Since the Sheriff is a state constitutional officer, the Legislature in Richmond determines how many deputies can be hired per 1,000 citizens. But the state constitution also provides that jurisdictions that want more protection than the Sheriff can provide, may fund and establish their own police departments. That is why, in many towns, cities and counties in Virginia, you will find both a police department and a Sheriff's Office. In Fairfax County, the police department is about three times the size of the Sheriff's Office and the Sheriff, despite having the same law enforcement powers as the police, generally restricts its responsibilities to securing the courthouse, running the jail and all correctional activities, serving civil process and executing orders of the court. I looked into a job as a deputy and found that the Sheriff's Office had about twenty part-time positions as court security officers, or, bailiffs. This made sense because misdemeanor criminal dockets and traffic courts, as well as general district civil court dockets, were extremely heavy in the morning, and as these case loads are dealt with, part-timers can be sent home to be replaced by full-time deputies. There was a very decent hourly wage attached to these part-time positions but there were no other benefits. Many of these positions were in fact filled by retired military and police officers. Part-timers were issued a handgun with which they must qualify, and then they were issued credentials and sworn in by the Clerk of the Court. All training, at that time, was by OJT.

I felt that a part-time job, especially one paying as well as this one did, might be all Janine and I needed. I applied for and was accepted as a part-time deputy. The first problem that developed with this part-time arrangement was that I loved the job and hated it when I was told to "Go 10-42." That's the law enforcement ten-series code for "out of service at home." I took all kinds of steps to stay on the clock as long as I could. I joined the Court Security Branch coffee fund but after my first cup in the morning, I never want back to the office where the supervisors might see me and send me home. Of course, one can't get away with evading for long and eventually "Go 10-42" will catch up to you.

In the meantime, Janine had to carry a bigger load with the kids as well as the store. During my year as a part-time deputy, an old acquaintance was also hired as a part-timer. This would be retired FBI Special Agent John House who interviewed me for a Special Agent's job in the Washington field office many years earlier. We got to be friends.

After over a year as a part-time deputy, I applied for full-time status, knowing that it meant shift work and that I would start in the county jail where every full time deputy starts. It would mean longer hours (lots) and more money (much). Additionally, as a full-time deputy, once I completed mandated academy training, I could participate in the promotional process to acquire more rank, which meant more pay.

In the summer of 1985, I attended the full course for new deputies and police officers at the Northern Virginia Criminal Justice Academy. The course was divided into the Basic and Combined Schools. All that meant was that police recruits in the Basic School would spend more time on subject matter dealing with things they would do, like traffic enforcement, while deputies in the Combined School would spend more time on things such as court security and jail operations. During my class, I was elected vice president and, at the end, was the honor graduate of the Combined School. I had already decided to compete in the promotional process at every opportunity no matter where the job was.

During my sixteen years as a full-time deputy, successive promotions put me in Supply, Administration, Training, Civil Process, back to the jail as a Confinement Squad supervisor, to the newly built Fairfax County Criminal Justice Academy as an Assistant Commander, then to Community Corrections (Work Release, Inmate Labor, Electronic Incarceration, Community Service) and then to the rank of major where I became the

Commander of the Community Corrections Division. My endless pursuit of promotions got me to the rank of major quickly where, like in the Army, I remained in that rank for many years. Unlike the Army, however, a major in the Fairfax County Sheriff's Office was a division commander.

I continued to love my job until January of 2000. What changed was in the November election of 1999, the incumbent Sheriff lost to a challenger. The challenger had been a friend of mine when he too was a Fairfax County Deputy Sheriff. He decided to run against the current Sheriff who then fired him. Firing this man, a single parent with custody of two young daughters, was not the smartest thing the incumbent Sheriff could do. The challenger picked up a lot of sympathy votes from people who ordinarily wouldn't even bother to vote in a sheriff's election and he won.

As the Sheriff-elect, he arranged to meet with each division commander, away from the jail/courthouse complex, and get a briefing on what each division was doing. During his meeting with me, the Sheriff-elect asked me to be his Chief Deputy Sheriff, holding the rank of lieutenant colonel. I had to think hard about this because through the rank of major, deputy sheriffs in Fairfax County had civil service protection and could not be fired at the pleasure of the Sheriff. That was not the case at the rank of lieutenant colonel. In Virginia, the state code states that no police chief or sheriff will wear an insignia of rank higher than that of the Superintendent of State Police, which is the eagle, and the rank of colonel.

A lieutenant colonel, second in command, could most definitely be fired at the pleasure of the Sheriff. I took a chance and told the new Sheriff that I would accept the Chief Deputy position. And that turned out to be a big mistake. The Sheriff didn't fire me and, in fact, asked me not to go when I told him I was retiring. The reason for retiring after a year on the job, to me, was simple. I always liked working with good people, young subordinates I could mentor and encourage and support in exchange for their best efforts on the job. When I took the chief's job, I had no good, hardworking subordinates. They all worked for other supervisors. All I dealt with were the unhappy and bad employees through the grievance and discipline process. Then there was a never ending series of inmate lawsuits alleging cruel and unusual punishment or medical malpractice. We never lost any of these lawsuits, but even though they were bullshit, we still had to go through pre-trial stuff such as discovery.

With my promotion to chief, I had moved up the pay schedule significantly and at the end of one year in this position, I could retire with the same pension I would have gotten had I stayed, retiring as a major with a full twenty years with the agency. Bottom line, I no longer liked my job and on December 31, 2000, I retired for a second time.

The 14 Karat Gift Shop had closed after our initial five year lease. The store always paid its own way but there wasn't much left over for us. Had Janine been able to hire someone who did jewelry repair, the store might have lasted longer. But, Janine got the retail store thing out of her system and it didn't make sense for her to spend six days a week in a place that wasn't contributing that much to our well-being. Shortly after she liquidated store inventory, fixtures, furnishings and equipment, she obtained her real estate license and began selling homes. Within six months of my retirement, I went to work at the NRA shooting range as a range safety officer. Then, after both Janine and I had our fill of working, we bought a thirty-seven foot diesel pusher motor home, sold our house and traveled around the country RVing for the next three years. After that, we sold the "bus," bought another home in Virginia and today alternately take vacations and cruises while watching our grandkids grow up.

Acknowledgments

S UPERIOR OFFICERS, SOLDIERS, FRIENDS AND some people I wasn't all that crazy about inspired me to write this book, although those in the last category are absolutely in the minority. First, I need to recognize the men I served with during my first combat tour in Vietnam, starting with my bosses with the RVN Airborne 5th Battalion advisory team: Captain Gerald "Tex" Sewell (last I heard, alive and well); Captain Mel Drisko (deceased); and Captain James Rogan (KIA). Next, is my best friend at the time, Team NCO Sergeant First Class John E. Milender (KIA).

Next, I want to recognize the men who served with me in Delta Company, 2d Battalion, 8th Cavalry Regiment, 1st Cavalry Division in Vietnam from October 1968 to May 1969. I thank them for the magnificent way they did their jobs in the unfriendly jungles of Vietnam, and I thank so many of them for being my friends today. Commanding Delta Company was the high point of my twenty-year military career, a period of seven months which I could never match for the remainder of that career.

I owe special thanks to a fellow Cavalry trooper who I met via email only within the past year, Leif Aamot. Leif served with the 5th of the 7th Cav about the same period of time that I was with the 2nd of the 8th. He was referred to me by another Angry Skipper 6, Bill Neal, who commanded D 2/8 in 1970. Leif contacted Bill seeking information about a fight in November 1968 in which his company was involved and Bill put him in touch with me. Delta

Company's fight in the same area being researched by Leif was a few days later and is covered in Chapter Nine, "Chicken Valley." Leif had been doing research in the military archives and once we made contact, he was able to provide me with copies of maps and duty logs which helped me greatly in writing *Company Grade*. I want to thank Colonel Robert Spiller, Chief of Staff of the U. S. Command, Berlin, who made my assignment there from 1978-1980 the second most memorable and enjoyable assignment of my career. From the minute I solved the Berlin Hunting Club's vexing problem of an arms room that failed to meet Army standards, Colonel Spiller became my greatest fan.

Not that I didn't make some good friends in these assignments, but I don't particularly need to thank anyone from Eighth U. S. Army, Korea, the Pentagon or the U. S. Army Military District of Washington.

I do need to thank my wife Janine who, although we didn't meet until after I finished my Vietnam duty, shared in many of my worst experiences in the war by way of nocturnal flashbacks that often sent her to the couch downstairs.

I retired in the summer of 1983 in order to help Janine open her gift and jewelry store, which she did. The store began immediately paying for itself with little left over in the way of income. That forced me to find another job, which I did, with the Fairfax County, Virginia, Sheriff's Office. That became a second career lasting seventeen years where I rose through the ranks from PFC through LTC. For that, I need to thank the three Sheriffs for whom I worked: M. Wayne Huggins, Carl R. Peed and Stan Barry.

Lastly, I need to thank my three sons, Erik, Chris and Mike, who continued to remind me that I was supposed to write a book and staying on my case until I did.

About the Author

H ENRY "ROCKY" COLAVITA served multiple tours in Vietnam. His first was as an adviser with the Vietnamese Airborne in 1965 and '66, and the second as a company commander with the 1st Cavalry Division in 1968 and '69. After twenty years he retired from the Army as a lieutenant colonel and was then hired by the Fairfax County, VA Sheriff's Office where, over the next seventeen years, he progressed through every rank from private to Chief Deputy Sheriff. He currently lives in Haymarket, VA.

CPSIA information can be obtained
at www.ICGtesting.com
Printed in the USA
LVOW04s0840030216
473413LV00016B/110/P